Captured by a Smile
"Imprisoned by Love"

Captured by a Smile
"Imprisoned by Love"

✦

A Memoir of Young Love that Refused to Die

D. W. Gutridge Sr.

iUniverse, Inc.
New York Lincoln Shanghai

Captured by a Smile
"Imprisoned by Love"

A Memoir of Young Love that Refused to Die

iUniverse books may be ordered through booksellers or by contacting:

iUniverse
1663 Liberty Drive
Bloomington, IN 47403
www.iuniverse.com
1-800-Authors (1-800-288-4677)

ISBN: 978-0-5954-7007-5 (pbk)
ISBN: 978-0-5957-0774-4 (cloth)
ISBN: 978-0-5959-1291-9 (ebk)

Printed in the United States of America

iUniverse rev. date: 10/24/2012

This book, of course, can only be dedicated to the person for whom it was written.

It gives me great pleasure to affectionately dedicate this book to my lovely wife, Jacqueline Dee Gutridge. I would also like to dedicate this book to our beautiful children, Stephanie, Tiffany, and Daniel Jr., and to our two grandchildren, Adrianna Chelsea-Marie, and Tobias Niles.

Contents

Introduction
To the Girl of My Dreams,
the Lovely Jackie Dee

This is the story of a young boy's endless love for that special girl who was revealed to him to be the girl of his dreams almost forty years ago. Anyone who reads this love story will see that there is something very special and unique about the relationship between Jackie Dee and Daniel; it is unlike anything you have ever read before. At first, I wasn't exactly sure where I should begin with our story. I have decided to start by sharing a little bit about my background before writing about my earliest memories of Jackie Dee, to whom hereafter—I will refer to as "the girl of my dreams," and our relationship.

The reasons behind sharing our story after some thirty years are many. First and foremost, I want to convey to the girl of my dreams my deepest, most heartfelt emotions, which I have never been able to share with her before. As you read our story, I think you will come to understand why.

Also, it is my hope that in writing this story—it will help me to cope with some of my twisted and perplexed emotions, which to this day has been causing me some problems in that at times I cannot think about anything else. These emotional twists and turns, both good and bad, have both inspired me and haunted me throughout our relationship. Up until just recently, I have always been able to keep myself so busy that I was able to suppress these emotions that I kept harbored inside of my heart. However, the resurfacing of theses emotions has increased more so now than ever before. Is this normal? I doubt it. Is this healthy? Probably not.

Lastly, this love story is an appeal. To see if there is anyone out there who can relate to what I've tried so desperately to express within these pages. In the process of telling my story, perhaps I will invoke some chords of emotions in others that will be instrumental in unlocking the mysteries behind this powerful emotion called love.

For years, a number of people—mostly my family and friends—have told me that I should write a book about my life story. However, I don't think this story is going to turn out anything like what they may have expected, due to the fact that I have never shared with anyone most of the things about which I have written here. I should forewarn you that I'm going to be very open, honest, and blunt concerning what I have to share about the perplexities of Jackie's and my relationship. This love story, with its many ups and downs, is so intriguing that it is truly worthy of being told.

And so, to the best of my ability, the story in its entirety is written from the standpoint of what _my mindset was_—at the time I experienced each occurrence of our relationship down through the years. In conclusion, be advised that this story does contain some strong language at times in an effort to render the story as accurately as humanly possible. What I've written will no doubt offend many, and for that, I apologize most sincerely. But I must tell our story as it happened, so I've refrained from sugarcoating it or watering it down in any way. Readers, beware.

This one is for you, Jackie Dee, the girl of my dreams.

1

It's a Wonderful Life

Before I get started on how Jackie Dee and I first met, I think it is important to touch briefly on my background and how I was raised. It is also important to talk about how the environment around me contributed to how I grew up.

Jackie Dee and I were both born and raised on Kansas City's east side during the late fifties and early sixties, a time when the Civil Rights Movement was just gaining momentum and when sex, drugs, and rock and roll were just about everybody's preoccupations. Our neighborhood was rapidly becoming tumultuous; some sort of violent crime took place in the city every day. In just a few short years, the area that we lived in went from bad to worse, and crime began to take over our neighborhood.

I remember watching a segment on the six o'clock news one day concerning a young woman who was stabbed to death at a bus stop a couple of blocks away from where we lived. Apparently, when her assailant confronted her, she refused to hand over the only money she had in her possession—her bus fare—and he murdered her for it. It was all that she had, and she put up a fight to keep it rather than give it away. I could not believe it; she lost her life over ten cents! When I was a young boy, this incident came to mind whenever I held a dime in my hand, and I would think of that young lady.

I lived on Chelsea Street with my mother and father, my older sister, and my three older brothers. Even though Mom and Dad both worked, they must not have made very much money. It's also possible that they had gotten themselves into such debt that they could not get out. Whatever the reason was, we were poor. My mother and father were hardly ever home to look after us, and so we were essentially left to raise and fend for ourselves. I remember our utilities being shut off from time to time. It seemed like there was never enough food to eat, and being hungry all the time.

I have given a lot of thought to whether I should include this next portion of the story. However, some things happened to me as a young boy that affected me in a negative way for the rest of my life, so I decided they warranted mentioning.

While we were living on Chelsea, I always wondered why I was the only one out of all of the kids in my family who had to attend a Catholic school. Looking back, I now believe it was because I was always getting into fights or trouble of some kind. As a result of this, I think my mom made me attend a parochial school for disciplinary purposes.

From the get-go, I had problems buying into the Catholic beliefs—there were too many rituals that one had to perform in order to even get God's attention, let alone his favor. Even as a young boy, I felt sure that if God did exist, then in His infinite wisdom, he could figure out an easy and painless way for man to reach out to Him if he so desired to. There had to be a better way than going through all the dark rituals and sacraments I was being indoctrinated with.

Another problem was that I refused to be intimidated by the priest or nuns and would never back down. The priest and nuns would use intimidation or fear on the other students to control and manipulate them into doing whatever they wanted them to do, but these things didn't work on me. Because of this, I (as well as others) had to endure slaps to the face, the occasional hair-pulling, and getting the heck shaken out of me by the shoulders. Occasionally, they would even trip us.

I once saw them tie one of my fellow students, Patrick, to his desk with a rope while they stood over him, taunting, and antagonizing him.

I also remember another incident that involved a little girl who sat in front of me in class. The little girl's name was Nancy.

She told me that she needed to use the restroom, but she was afraid to ask. Thus, I raised my hand.

When the nun finally acknowledged my raised hand, I asked her, "Could Nancy please be allowed to use the restroom?"

The nun responded in a loud voice, "She is a child of God, let her ask for herself."

However, Nancy would not ask until she finally could not hold it any longer, and then she raised her hand. The nun purposely acted as if she did not see Nancy's raised hand, so I cleared my throat loudly enough that she would have to look our way. When the nun saw the little girl's hand, she said, "What is it?"

Nancy began to shake and started to cry as she asked the nun if she could use the restroom. The nun told Nancy that she would have to wait until lunch break, which was still half an hour away. But Nancy couldn't wait any longer and began to wet on herself as she sat there in her desk, afraid to move a muscle. As the urine hit the floor right there in front of me, I had to jump up out of my seat to keep from getting any of it on me. From across the room, the nun hollered at me to get back in my seat. As a rule, you were not supposed to get out of your seat without permission. I stood in the back of the classroom with my arms folded and would not get back into my seat. Nancy's urine was now pooling right where my feet would be situated had I remained seated at my desk.

Even when I was a young boy, I never had any problems speaking my mind. As I stood in the back of the classroom in the presence of the entire class, I told the nun that what she had done was wrong and that she should have allowed Nancy to use the restroom. The nun became so upset with me that her face turned bright red, and she started yelling at me, but I could not make out exactly what she was saying. It sounded like she said, "I've had it with you, you'll be punished, you'll be sorry!"

The nun ran over to where I was standing and grabbed me with one hand while she slapped me in the face and on the head with the other. I tried to block what slaps I could, but I was only eight or nine years old at the time. She tried physically forcing me back into my seat, but I would not cooperate and kept resisting her the best I could. She finally gave up and said she was going to get one of the priests. Then I knew I was in trouble, because the priests did not always hit you with an open hand, but sometimes with their fists. Some of the girls and boys started crying as the nun left the room, although I'm not exactly sure why they were crying; I was the one in trouble, not them.

Just then, I remembered how the nuns and the priest had tied Patrick up with ropes that one time. I looked across the room at the open window and decided that rather than wait for the nun and priest to return, I would run and dive out the window, which is exactly what I did. There was only about a six-foot drop on the other side. I hit the ground like a tumbler, rolled to my feet, and started walking down the street, thinking what a relief it was to be away from all of them. At least for the time being anyway, I was free from all their tyrannical bullshit.

I skipped school the next day, and when I returned to school the following day, the nuns did not say anything to me. I thought God must have performed a miracle; I had thought I would at least receive some kind of punishment for getting out of my seat without permission, not to mention leaving the school grounds. Then again, they may have been fearful of what I might have said to my parents about the whole matter concerning Nancy.

The fact was, I hadn't told them anything; I never told my parents or any of my family about my problems at school or in my life in general. We were not a close family; in fact, I did not feel close to anybody. Growing up, I felt like I had no one I could talk to or confide in, and so I would always try to weather the hard things in life by myself. Sometimes, two or three days would go by without my even seeing either one of my parents. When they did see me, they must have seen cuts and bruises on me all the time, but I suppose they just figured I had fallen out of a tree or off a roof or something, which were things I sometimes did.

Once there was an incident in school, in which one of the nuns discovered that some money she had stashed under a bell on her desk was missing. She strip-searched almost everyone in the classroom before she got the money back from the little girl who had taken it. I do not know what kind of punishment the little girl received for taking the money, but the staff and students did not treat her very kindly after that. Even though I was young and naive concerning the ways of the world, I still knew in my heart that what they had done to us was wrong. We were forced to endure embarrassments like this more than once. Sometimes they would put their hands on my private area while searching me, and they would also do this at other times to tell me to go use the restroom.

One of the rituals in which the students and parishioners had to fulfill was the sacrament of penance. This consisted of the confession of ours sins "both mortal and venial" to the priest, otherwise known as the Father, in these small enclosed stalls called confessional booths. I always thought this was kind of an odd ritual in that sins could be absolved by whatever penance was imposed by the priest. In my case, the penance was usually reciting the Our Father and Hail Mary hundreds of times while marching around the inside of the church. I know you are probably thinking that doesn't sound like much of an imposing penance for anyone to have to perform, but for the most part, I had to recite the prayers while marching around the church pews on my knees. I thought, "So this is what it takes to earn God's forgiveness? Possessing a penitent heart while wearing out the knees of my trousers until both of my knees are a bloody mess?" I always wondered, "Then why in God's creation was Christ crucified?" Wasn't it supposed to be for the absolution of our sins?

One Saturday afternoon in October of 1968, some of my friends and I planned a little outing. We would walk about two miles to an area where we could do some rock climbing. Close by was a salvage yard where we could play around with some of the damaged and wrecked vehicles, and there was also a nearby gas station that sold cigarettes for twenty cents a pack—I having picked the habit up since the second grade.

One of the boys that were going with us on this outing had a younger brother. Their parents had instructed the younger brother that he was never to leave the yard when they were away from the house. Such was the case on this particular Saturday morning. But the younger brother put up such a fuss about wanting to come with us that I stood up for him and insisted that he should be able to go on the outing. The other boys argued with me furiously, but to no avail; I would not back down, even to the point of throwing a few punches to drive my point home.

There were five of us, and we made the two-mile journey to where the hills and the salvage yard were located. We wore ourselves out on the rocks, climbing around on them all day long, and ending up at the salvage yard. Then we began messing around with some of the abandoned cars. One of them was a Corvair vehicle that was lying on its side. Since I was the leader of this little outfit, I told everybody that when we could push this vehicle over one way or the other, then we could begin our trek homeward.

We could not get the vehicle to tip either way until I found an old drive shaft that we could use as a pry bar. We positioned it under the vehicle as far as it would go. Then all of us grabbed hold of the makeshift pry bar and began to lift it in one concentrated effort, much like the U.S. Marines did when they lifted the standard that hoisted the American flag over Iwo Jima. The car began to move, and as we continued to lift, over she finally went, glass breaking and metal popping. We were so excited about our accomplishment that we felt like we could achieve anything, and we jumped up and down and yelled for joy. That soon gave way to exhaustion, as we had spent the whole day rock climbing and playing around in the salvage yard. We were all filthy messes.

We purchased some cigarettes for twenty cents a pack, which kids could do in those days, and then we began our long walk home.

I told everybody to pick up any empty pop bottles they happened to find along the side of the road—we could cash the empty bottles in for money at a local convenience store on our way. With the money, we could each buy a soda and a candy bar. We were all so thirsty that we stopped at a local park and drank from a public water fountain that ran continuously.

As we headed for the store to cash in the pop bottles we had found, I noticed that we had begun to spread out, the longer-legged kids pulling ahead of the younger kids in our group. By the time I made it to the store, we were quite spread out, and the youngest one, the one who wasn't supposed to leave the yard, the one whom I insisted be able to go, was at least a block behind us. I went into the store and stood in line to cash in the empty pop bottles. When I turned to my right and looked out the storefront window, I saw the youngest boy begin to cross the street between two parked cars. When he stepped out from between the cars to cross, he was struck by a speeding vehicle.

I dropped everything I was carrying and ran out into the busy street; cars swerved around me, missing me by only inches. I found myself in the same spot where I'd witnessed the impact occur. As I looked down at the pavement, I could see the little boy's shoes lying in the street. The car had struck him with such force that it had knocked the shoes right off his feet. It was determined later that the vehicle that had struck the little boy had been traveling more than fifty miles per hour in a thirty-five mile-per-hour speed zone.

I turned to my left and looked up the street; eighty-three feet away from the point of impact, where I was standing, lay the young boy who had accompanied us on what had now turned into a most horrific day. I ran to the spot where he was lying, and as the young boy looked up at me, his eyes began to grow dim and he struggled for his last breath of air. I watched his eyes close for the last time, and I heard all the air expel from his lungs. I saw the blood stop flowing from the chest and head injuries he had sustained from the impact.

I stood there and looked down at my friend laying in the street, this boy who'd literally had the life knocked right out of him. At that moment, I realized that I couldn't have been more responsible for his death if I had pushed him in front of the speeding vehicle myself. I wanted more than anything to be the one lying there dead instead of this little boy, who had barely begun to live his life.

Emergency personnel tried in vain to revive and save my friend, but he was gone forever. I couldn't believe it; because of my own actions, I now lived in a world in which my friend no longer existed. I wanted to go to sleep somehow and wake up later to find that this all had been a terrible dream—but it was not.

Never mind the excuse that I was only ten years old; I was still in control and very much responsible for everything that took place that day. I never did buy into the fact that being young was a valid excuse that people often cling to in order to exonerate themselves for their actions. If we are not responsible or accountable for our actions, then who is—Father Time?

For days after this tragedy, I could not be calmed, comforted, or even restrained. I was in such a state of hysteria that I could not even attend my friend's funeral. I remained in a state of shock for days, and the weeks that followed. This incident, to say the least, crushed and devastated me in such a heart- and gut-wrenching way that I still have not been able to forgive myself to this very day. I feel like a part of my heart completely shut down and died on that god-awful day of October 26, 1968.

At no time did anyone ever point the finger of blame at me, but I knew damn well that I was responsible for the loss of that six-year-old boy's life. His name was Johnny; he was my friend. When this little boy passed away, I felt like I had wiped out an entire universe of dreams, hopes, aspirations, and memories—everything, gone. The sky seemed to be gray for days after this incident, and I felt that God had turned his back on me and that forgiveness would not be forthcoming.

I felt that God simply did not love me anymore, if he ever had.

I have never shared the details of this god-awful tragedy with anyone before because it is so painful for me to recount. Nevertheless, this incident no doubt affected me from that day forth in a very negative way. At the time, I did not care if I lived to see another day. I felt like I had laid the foundation for my path to destruction.

A year or so later, after one of my altar boy rehearsals, I was supposed to attend practice for an upcoming play. I was probably eleven or twelve years old at the time. I was running late that Friday afternoon, and when I finally made it to the practice, I could tell that one of the nuns was cross with me because of my tardiness. God only knows why I had been the only boy chosen for this play. Girls, who tended to have a mystifying effect on me—I could not be myself around them or even think clearly—surrounded me.

When it came time for my part, the nuns signaled me to recite my lines, so I opened my mouth, but nothing came out. I was petrified, surrounded by all those little girls. Just then, the nun who was cross with me for being late walked over and stood in front of me, and then she slapped me across the face. She slapped me so hard that I began to see stars. I put my hand on my face; I could feel welts forming caused by the spacing between her fingers when she had struck me, and something inside of me snapped. Without hesitation, I swung my right fist and punched the nun in the stomach. I hit her so hard that it knocked her headdress right off. You could hear all the air rush out of her stomach and lungs as she tried to catch her breath.

While the nun I had punched was doubled over, the other nuns ran off to fetch one of the priests. Some of the girls who were standing close by pointed their fingers at me and said I was going to hell for what I had done. However, none of that seemed to matter just then; what did matter was the fact that now I knew that these nuns were just like anybody else and that they could be hurt. I got so excited about that thought that I hit the nun again. The second punch sent her to the floor, and everybody fled the room.

The priest showed up in a flash and ordered me to help the nun up off the floor. I thought, "Doesn't that figure, it would have to be the priest who had arms that looked like tree trunks show up. I refused to help her up, not wanting to take my eyes off him. The priest helped her up and out the door, and then he returned closing and locking the door behind him. There were no open windows for me to dive out of in this room.

Before he started letting me have it, he told me that God was going to chastise me through him and that he was just an instrument of God, our Father. He then proceeded to give me one of the worst beatings I had ever received in my life. I remember throwing punches around and fighting back the best I could, but I only succeeded in making matters worse for myself. I had thought that my brothers and my dad hit hard, but I think this son of a bitch broke my jaw—it would not close properly. It has been more than thirty-five years since all this happened, and I still have problems closing my mouth properly sometimes when I chew or yawn. By the time he was done with me, the roof of my mouth was split and a couple of my teeth were loose, but I never loss consciousness. I could also feel a couple of knots forming on my head, and I believe he must have cracked a rib or two because my left side hurt for the longest time afterward. When he was finished, I remember lying on the floor crying, spitting up blood, and vomiting. The whole thing probably did not last more than a couple of minutes, but it sure seemed like a long time.

As I lay there on the floor, I told that priest, "I swear to you, when I'm older, I'm going to come back here, and it's going to be your ass on the receiving end of my lefts and rights, may God our Father help you!"

The priest said, "Be still, my son."

As I lay there crying, I said, "I'm not your damn son, and when you die, I'm going to piss on your grave!"

That remark earned me another backhand, but by that point in time, I really did not care. I kept looking around the room for something to bash his damn skull in.

As I said before, there would sometimes be periods of two or three days during which I would not see either my mom or my dad. Such was the case after this particular incident, and when my parents finally saw me several days later, they figured I had fallen out of a tree or gotten roughed up by one of my brothers or one of the kids in the neighborhood, because I was always getting into fights.

When I returned to school that following Monday, I had started carrying a pocketknife. It had a very sharp, three-inch blade, and I would not hesitate to use it if I felt it was necessary.

Not long after this incident, a couple of the nuns came to the house to speak to my parents about my behavioral problems and some of my other issues. They advised my parents that I should start attending a different school the following year, but they said nothing about the incident that had occurred during play rehearsal. I think they may have been afraid to say anything because of what I could have told my parents about the physical abuse I had suffered at the hands of one of their own.

After the nuns left the house that day, my mom was extremely upset by what they had said about my usage of foul language, my behavioral problems, the fact I occasionally skipped school and lacked respect for the organization as a whole. In her anger, she grabbed a steel dustpan from the kitchen pantry and began hitting me with it. I put my arms up to block the incoming swings, and one of the corners of the steel dustpan stuck in my elbow.

Anyway, I survived the rest of that school year without incident. And let me tell you, the nuns were a little leery of coming near me for the rest of that year, especially the nun who had slapped me.

Not long after that school year ended, they tore that Catholic school down and replaced it with a parking lot for a newly constructed apartment complex—amen!

The next school year, I started attending a public school for the first time in my young life. It was a culture shock for me, to say the least. There were no dark, morning rituals, no penguins lurking about, and no pedophile priests putting their damn hands on us. Most importantly, though, there was no bullshit religion to be indoctrinated with.

I struggled with whether I should mention this difficult portion of my life, but I felt it was necessary for my readers to understand the psychological effects it would have on me for the rest of my life. I would have difficulties from time to time dealing with my own self-worth, and so I felt that explaining my background could help to better understand my story. I suffered physical abuse and some sexual abuse, but the worst was the verbal abuse. Plenty of other students had to endure these types of abuse on a regular basis as well. I still remember the names of all the priests and nuns and the names of all the students whom I witnessed suffering the same abuses and humiliations that I did. The institution from top to bottom made me feel inadequate in so many ways that I began to doubt my inherent self-worth. To sum things up, I came away from there believing that something was wrong with me.

All I had been through had scarred me so badly that in my mind—that is, my intellectual mind—I doubted whether God, Jesus, Mary, or any other deity—so called had ever existed to begin with. On the other hand, somewhere in the recesses of my heart, I knew that there had to be a loving, kind, and caring God out there somewhere, but where? Hell, as depraved as I was rapidly becoming, even I could look on creation and know there had to be a design architect behind all the beauty that was in the world. And when I saw Jackie Dee for the first time, I absolutely knew without a doubt that there had to be a God.

As bad as things were at school, things back at home were not much better. For the most part, we wore hand-me-down clothes.

Two of my brothers and I had to sleep on a straw mattress with steel springs that lay on a carpeted, concrete floor in a room that had no heat or even heating vents. My older brothers would make me sleep on the part of the mattress where some of these steel springs were sticking through. On occasion, we would have to cut back the protruding wires with pliers to keep them from impaling us.

When I woke up one morning, I thought I had wet the bed, even though I had never done this before. I got up out of bed and came into the light, where I could see. I looked down and saw that my underwear was covered in blood. One of the sharp springs had gouged me in a most embarrassing spot—my behind—and I clearly needed stitches. The cut was about two inches long, and it felt pretty deep. You are not going to believe this, but my mom and dad duct-taped the wound closed and sent me off to school.

That morning, I gingerly walked to school, which was only a couple of blocks away from where I lived. With each step I took, the pain in my rear grew worse and worse. When I finally arrived at my classroom, the teacher told me to take a seat, but I pretended I was being stubborn and unruly and refused to take a seat. In reality, I could not sit down for the pain I was in.

My teacher said, "Fine, if you don't want to sit down, then you can just stand in the back of the classroom until you are ready to take a seat."

I was too embarrassed to say anything about the matter to her, so I stood in the back of the classroom all day, which seemed like forever. I still have a large scar on my rear end to this day.

As a child, I frequently suffered from nosebleeds. When I started attending public school, I was pleased that my teachers would always send me to the school's clinic, where a nurse would be standing by to attend to me. By contrast, the Catholic school's protocol for dealing with these nosebleeds was quite different. As matter of fact, I do not believe we had a nurse; I don't remember ever seeing one. Instead, if my nose started bleeding, they would tell me to tilt my head back and just sit there. If it continued to bleed, then so be it, at least until our next recess period or lunch break, when I could attend to it properly and clean it up myself.

From my youth through early adulthood, whether I was sleeping or awake, I would sometimes suffer from nosebleeds so severe that I would have to lie still for close to an hour in an effort to stop the bleeding. I always thought these nosebleeds were the direct result of an incident that happened to me when I was very young.

One day when I was around five or six years old, several of us kids were broad-jumping off a porch and across some concrete blocks. Broad-jumping is where you leap with both feet simultaneously in the air for height and distance. The porch belonged to a woman who was babysitting me at the time. We were having a contest to see who could broad-jump to the farthest concrete block. The porch was only about five feet high, but to a small child, it sure seemed like it was much taller.

As I began to make my attempt to jump, one of the other kids shoved me in the back just as I was pushing off. I went straight up into the air, then spun and landed on the top of my head, striking the corner of one of these concrete blocks. The next thing I remember was waking up while being driven to the hospital. I was lying across a man and a woman in the front seat of a car with my legs and feet in the man's lap and my head in the lap of the woman.

I had a splitting headache so severe that it felt like my head was trapped in a vice as it was being tightened. I could barely see out of my left eye, and my right eye was completely swollen shut. Out of my squinted left eye, I could see my blood all over these people. I didn't know at the time who these people were, but I remember the young lady crying over and over again, "Please, God, don't let this little boy die; please, God, don't let him die." I would find out later, that they were the parents of the boy who had pushed me.

I received a great many stitches on the right side of my forehead, where there is still a noticeable scar to this day. I do not know if this accident had anything to do with my nosebleeds or not, but it sure seemed like they happened with greater frequency after I fell.

Interestingly enough, being the youngest of four boys (at least for the first ten years of my life), I also got the extra bonus of bearing the abuse that is usually associated with being the youngest. You know, the usual—having your teeth twisted out with pliers, being shocked with an electrical lamp cord, and the good ol' punch or kick in the jaw or head. My favorite was being used as a moving target for BB gun practice.

As if I hadn't already been through enough in the first twelve years of my life, there was also an incident in which I was attacked by a police dog while playing football in a nearby vacant lot. The vacant lot was situated on the corner of 24th and Chelsea Street. A man who trained dogs for the Kansas City Police owned the house next to the vacant lot. One dog was tethered to a doghouse by a thick log chain. The dog attacked me just as I was being tackled; my opponent drove me down into the gravel driveway just far enough that the police dog could lunge at me and initiate that first bite right on top of my head. Then the dog began to backpedal, dragging me across the driveway by my head.

As my blood began to squirt in all different directions, the dog began to shake me so violently that I thought my neck was going to break. I began punching the dog with my fist, which caused him to release me momentarily, but then he bit me on top of the head again, and this time he had an even better hold on me. All I could see was the color red, as my eyes were full of the blood that was running down from my head. The kids were all crying and screaming for someone to come and help.

With all my might, I continued punching the dog, and then I began to yank my head and body backwards in an almost tug-of-war-like fashion. The dog released me and I rolled backwards away from him, head over heels, just far enough that I was beyond his reach when his chain was fully extended. The dog was growling viciously at me, his snout literally just inches away from my blood-covered face. Bleeding profusely, the neighborhood kids weeping and wailing all around me, I rose to my feet and staggered down Chelsea Street in the opposite direction from where I lived.

With my fingers, I could feel flaps of my torn scalp barely hanging on. I took off my blood-soaked shirt and covered my head in an effort to stop the bleeding or at least try and slow it down. All I can remember saying is, "My dad is going to kill me; my dad is going to kill me."

Ironically enough, it was my dad who found me; someone informed him of what had happened to me, and he drove me to the hospital. The doctor applied numerous amounts of stitches in an effort to suture and piece my ripped-up scalp back together again.

For months prior to this attack, the neighborhood kids had been throwing rocks and sticks at this dog every time they walked by, antagonizing him and causing him to become vicious. The dog was never put to sleep for the attack; instead, he was sold to a shop owner whose store was on 24th Street. This meant that I had to walk past the dog to go to and from school every day. The dog would lunge at the big, plate glass window nearly hard enough to break it whenever anyone walked by. This dreadful incident took place when I was just twelve years old, and I will never forget it for as long as I live.

Well, as if things couldn't get any tougher growing up, I didn't fair any better in elementary school or high school. There was no such a thing as middle school back then, but I am sure it wouldn't have made any difference. To me, elementary school was just a prelude to worse things to come in high school. In grade school, the students, rather than fight me hand to hand, would try and stabbed me with pencils and on occasion would have books thrown at me. But while I was in high school, I was cut with knives a number of times during fistfights that broke out in the hallways. One day, I was stabbed in the ribcage while trying to use the restroom.

During one of the school riots—and believe me, there were a few—a teacher was thrown out a second-story window. The teacher survived the fall, but his back was broken, and he had a few other injuries as well.

I also once witnessed a mob of students turn a school bus over on its side while trying to get their hands on a student who was on the bus. The mob was after this student because he had raped a female student out back behind the school, then boasted about it to others that day. When word of it got around, some students took up the cause and went after him. Before the police had even arrived, they had beaten him half to death.

One time, I remember someone throwing several sticks of dynamite into the vestibule area of the library and blowing the entranceway doors off the hinges. The explosion caused some other damage as well—it shattered a lot of glass and so forth. When the riots became too uncontrollable for the local law enforcement agencies to handle, the National Guard had to come take control of the situations and try to restore order and keep the peace. They would always use tear gas on the students in an effort to disperse the crowds. In those days, there was no such thing as a safe learning environment for us. A riot could break out at any time. You never knew what you were going to walk into when you came to school each day and entered the classrooms. So much for an ideal, pleasant learning experience.

In addition to my home life and my problems at school, there was also a tremendous amount of civil tension with which we had to contend in those days. Fights broke out in my neighborhood all the time; there were stabbings, shootings, and the occasional riot in the streets. I can even remember a curfew order that was in effect for what seemed like the longest time. Such was my life on the east side of Kansas City. You really had to stay sharp and focused while going about your business, or you might just have ended up dead somewhere; it was that bad.

Anyway, I digress. Now, on to something so very much more pleasant.

2

Is There Such a Thing as a Life-Changing Smile?

My earliest memories of Jackie Dee date back to 1968 or 1969 and take place on Kansas City's east side. This would put Jackie at five or six years old and me around ten or eleven.

Up until this point in time, I'd had absolutely no interest in girls other than someone with whom to play hide-and-seek or tag. I would often see Jackie in those days, walking, skipping, and jumping around 24th Street between Chelsea and Lister. She was usually in the company of a tall woman, though sometimes she was with a shorter woman who seemed not much taller than I was. I learned a year or two later that the tall woman was Jackie's mother and that the shorter woman was her aunt. At the time, I didn't know where Jackie lived, but I saw her every now and again around Chelsea Street, which was the street that I lived on.

My friends were mostly boys my age, and there were some girls with whom I ran around the neighborhood. I later found out that one of these girls was Jackie's sister, but I never saw the two of them together. I only mention this because none of the girls with whom I ran and played struck any chord of emotion in me whatsoever, and why would they? I was so young.

As a young boy, I always tried to shy away from girls; they were a mystery to me, and I felt uncomfortable just being around them. They were built differently from me, and they smelled different from us boys. They generally could not run as fast, hit as hard, or climb trees very well.

What I remember most about seeing, or I should say glimpses of Jackie Dee in those days was thinking that she was very cute. She always seemed to be in motion, and she never stood still long enough for me to really get a good look at her. I must admit that even then I could sense that there was some-thing very special about Jackie, but I could not quite put my finger on what it was. Then came the day that my life was for-ever changed—the day that I actually got my first real, good look at this cute, little girl, Jackie Dee. That is, a good look from across the street anyway.

I was walking up the sidewalk on the side of the street that I lived on when I saw Jackie standing on the sidewalk with some friends. Then it happened: as Jackie turned her head in my direction, I saw her smile. It was not a full grin, mind you; it was just kind of a passing half smile, but it was enough to stop me right in my tracks.

No, she was not smiling at me; I don't even think she saw me standing there. But when I saw her smile, it was like she had a glow around her so bright that I couldn't make out if the kids standing next to her were boys, girls, aliens, or what. Nor did I even care; because of what I was beholding and what I was beginning to feel happening inside of me.

Not only did she possess this infectious darling of a smile, but she also had such long, golden, honey-blonde hair that flowed down over her tanned shoulders in such a carefree and innocent way. I had seen pretty girls before, but this was something entirely different.

Then something truly amazing began to happen to me. In that moment, over and over again in my mind's eye, I could see Jackie Dee and me years later. The best description I can offer of what I remember seeing is that we were in some kind of dream-like sequence, affectionately holding each other. Furthermore, in this dream or vision, we were both very nicely dressed, and we appeared to be very happy together.

I was never one to daydream, but believe me, this was no daydream. I know it sounds crazy, and looking back, I can hardly believe it myself, especially since I had never experienced anything like it before. Nevertheless, it did happen. At the time, I didn't know how old we were in this vision or if we were married or something. But I do know that we were together in every sense of what that word—together—meant and that we seemed to be very happy. Call it a glimpse into our future, or call it some kind of dream or vision—take your pick.

Anyway, from that day forth, my life was forever changed. All of a sudden, I was uncontrollably drawn to Jackie Dee by something that was completely beyond my understanding and reasoning and still baffles me to this day. Now, I know that the imagination is strong in a young boy, but this was something completely different. For the life of me, I cannot find the words to explain it; and there is nothing within the realm of knowledge or at least logic that can explain it either.

Little did Jackie Dee know that from that day forth, she would not only have possession of my heart, but she would also have me wrapped around her little finger for as long as I had a breath of life in me. And believe me, you haven't read anything yet; it gets steadily worse, depending on your point of view.

I remember that all of this took place around the time my grandmother passed away. That would put me at twelve years old; my grandmother passed away on my twelfth birthday.

Even at the time, I wondered how this could happen to such a stubborn, mule-headed, young boy like me, all in the twinkling of an eye. It all stemmed from Jackie Dee's captivating smile as she stood there across the street from me. This moment was the closest thing to an out-of-body experience that I would ever have in my life; time seemed to be standing still, as I was swept off my feet and carried away. I didn't know then what I was seeing in this little girl's smile, but I know now that what I beheld was heaven.

Standing there on that day, I knew with all my heart that from that day forth, Jackie Dee would be the girl of my dreams. The course of my whole life was determined by this one amazing event.

At no fault of my own did I do anything to bring this on. I did not ask for this—it just happened.

I had never experienced anything like it before, but the flood of emotions kept rushing through my heart, and the vision of Jackie and me being together kept flashing before me in my mind's eye. I had no idea what to make of this explosion of emotions that was taking place inside of me. Nevertheless, they overwhelmed me repeatedly, wave after wave, as I remained standing there.

Words fail me in trying to describe what it felt like, but here goes. While I was standing there and beholding this cute, little girl with the heavenly smile, it felt like something spectacularly wonderful was forming and welling up inside of me. It was as if my heart were doing summersaults inside of my chest.

Looking back, I believe that one of the things I was experiencing in my heart was love. For the first time in my life, I felt pure love—love for another individual. I suddenly found that I had the capacity to love Jackie Dee in a manner that did not exist within me before that very moment when I saw her smile. But now it was beginning to take root deep inside of me.

Is there anyone out there who can understand or relate to what happened to me or tell me why it happened then, when Jackie and I were so very young?

For the life of me, I wanted to cross that street and get a closer look at this cute, little girl who was causing all this commotion in both my heart and my mind. However, I could not take that first step; it was as if something were preventing me, as if it were not yet time for us to meet. Maybe it was my own inhibitions and shyness, or maybe it was something else.

Somehow, I knew her name was Jackie Dee; I'm not quite sure how I knew this, but I have a theory. I believe that an angel must have whispered her name to me in a dream as I lay sleeping one night.

I could literally write volumes about Jackie Dee's smile, which had such an astonishing effect on me, but I will try to tone it down for now so that I can get on with the rest of our story. I stood there in a daze across the street from this cute little girl with this darling of a smile for what seemed like a long time, but it was probably only for about a minute or two.

I have never shared this experience with anyone before right now, not even with Jackie Dee herself. As you read this story, I think you will understand why I held all of this inside for all those years. Who would have believed it anyway when I could hardly believe it myself? But it did happen.

Ironically enough, as I was standing there—I'd forgotten where I was even going. Anyway, I needed to find a place to hide and get a handle on things, so I quickly headed for home to try to sort things out. As I began to assess what had just taken place, I categorized my vision of Jackie's and my future as a promise of what was to come.

With my emotions still skyrocketing ever upward and out of control and thoughts of this promise or dream running through my mind, I found it impossible to think about anything else no matter how hard I tried. I was not in any way trying to rid myself of the emotions I was feeling for Jackie; to the contrary, I was merely trying to gain some kind of control over my heart and mind, as I was feeling a tremendous amount of anxiety. I literally felt the urge to shout what I was feeling for Jackie from the rooftops, but my God, we were so very young, and I knew even then that people would rightly perceive this as most peculiar. Why were these emotional bolts of lightning striking me down now, rather than at a more reasonable age?

Rather than resist the love and new emotions that I was feeling for Jackie, I came to embrace them. First of all, I was amazed by how remarkable it made me feel in my heart just to think of her and then how extraordinarily powerfully these emotions had begun to change my heart, my mind, and my whole outlook on life. It was like some kind of profound awareness was sweeping over me.

I am not trying to convince anybody of anything here, because in the grand scheme of things, it really doesn't matter what anyone else thinks about my dreams or me. What really does matter is what I know I experienced on that day and what

I think and believe about myself. As I stated before, at no fault of my own did I do anything to bring this on. I did not ask for this—it just happened.

Anyway, I digress. I found out later that Jackie lived with her mother and sister and that her mother was divorced, so she had no father figure in the early days of this story.

Having given a little bit of my background on how I was raised, then suddenly being awestruck by this darling, little girl name Jackie Dee and her angelic smile. Coupled with the thought that one-day we would be together; after all, this whole experience was happening to a boy who had only known hardship and abuse.

Being the matter-of-fact person that I was, I wanted quick confirmation on this whole matter, so I thought, "Let's see what happens when I see Jackie Dee again." Not many days later, I saw her again from across 24th Street, and I swear it felt like something was gripping and squeezing my heart tighter and tighter.

What in God's name was going on with me? And to think that this all started with her adorable smile that wasn't even directed at me—or was it?

Every time I saw Jackie Dee after that, I could feel my heart pulsating and moving around inside me. That was proof enough for me that I was being emotionally drawn to her and—to put it another way—my love for her. Yes, the emotions that had engulfed me were truly genuine, and this was real, as real as the very sidewalk I was standing on or the trees I could see bending in the wind on our street that day.

This was all the confirmation I would ever need.

3

A Life on Hold

Once again, I was all too aware of our ages—after all, we were just kids. The fact that a young boy could be so love-struck by a beautiful, little girl is just one of the reasons why this story is so fantastic. This was not your usual case of puppy love or some teenage crush. It was an all-out, head-over-heels, can't-sleep-at-night, can't-think-about-anything-else kind of love.

After giving this new, profound experience a considerable amount of thought, I devised a plan to try to put my emotions on hold if possible. I would try to wait at least until Jackie was a teenager before I would even think about letting her know I was interested in her. Then I would drop a hint here and there, if I could even manage that. I was always a strong-willed person and could show great restraint when I felt it was necessary, but this was really going to put me to the test.

My problem was that interacting with girls was the hardest thing for me socially. I mean, girls: come on—yikes! When I was around girls, I felt like a social misfit. I was so very shy, I could never be myself, and I had no idea what to say or how to act. It was terrifying for me. I hoped that as time passed and as I waited for the right moment to let Jackie know that I existed, I would be able to overcome some of my shyness. Maybe I could even learn something about how to conduct myself around girls, as I saw some of my friends do, without coming off like a complete idiot.

Sometime around 1970, as fate would have it, beautiful little Jackie Dee, who had my heart and head in such a swirl, moved just a few houses up the street from me. I would see her riding her bike or walking down Chelsea Street every now and again, and yes, my emotions would sometimes get the best of me. I had always wanted to say something—anything—to Jackie, but because of our age difference, I held back from saying anything more than just "Hi there."

One time, Jackie was riding her bicycle on the sidewalk and stopped in front of my friend's house, where I was standing and talking to him. This was the closest I had ever been to her. Jackie was even more beautiful up close than she was from across the street. This time, I was close enough that I could look right into her hazel-colored eyes and see that precious gleam in her smile that I'd seen the first time. In that moment, unable to keep from staring, I almost said to her, "You are one cute little girl," but something stopped me about halfway through. Standing this close to her, I could detect a lovely fragrance that was coming from her and filling the air around me, and it literally began to make me dizzy.

Jackie Dee had such a bold and lively personality that she just came right out and started telling my friend and me all about her grandma, who owned lots of land in Stover, Missouri. She went on to tell us that her grandma also owned a Laundromat that was just up the street and around the corner at 24th and Lister. This explained why I sometimes saw Jackie up on 24th Street between Chelsea and Lister, the next block over. Jackie's grandma also owned a house that was about a block and a half down the other side of 24th at Chelsea.

I'm not sure what I said to Jackie that day, but I am sure it didn't make any sense. With all that was happening inside me, my mind was anything but clear. As matter of fact, my mind was in an all-out fog, and a London fog at that.

After my first encounter and conversation with Jackie Dee that day, I turned to my friend and said, "She has got to be the cutest little girl I have ever seen." I could not believe what had just come out of my mouth and that I had shared what I was thinking with my friend. It was definitely a spontaneous reaction, but nothing stopped me from saying exactly what I wanted to say when I was ready to say it.

Some time after our first encounter, I saw Jackie singing and playing around in her front yard as I walked by the front of her house.

The house that Jackie lived in was on the same side of the street that I lived on and was just five houses up the street from me. As I was walking by her house, I could hear her singing, "Oh ... Daniel, oh ... Daniel." I thought, "Wow—she knows my name, and she's even singing it." As I walked by, I simply said to her, "Well, hello there," and went on by.

In 1972 through 1974, all the kids who lived on Chelsea Street would sometimes get together to play games in the street like tag or hide and seek, and sometimes Jackie Dee and I would participate. You have no idea how exciting this was for me; it gave me opportunities to see her up close and possibly even stand next to her. I had to try not to let anyone—especially Jackie catch me staring or even looking at her. Because of our age difference, I still kept any conversation with Jackie to a minimum. But when we played hide and seek, there were a few times that Jackie and I ran off into the night together and hid in the same spot. One place we hid together was on the rooftop of my next-door neighbor's garage, which was really a jaunt from home base. It felt so good to be that close to her in the dark recesses of the night, hidden away from everybody, that to this day just thinking about it sends chills down my spine.

You have no idea how hard it was for me not to be able to share what was happening to me emotionally with anyone, including Jackie. However, at the time I feared being made fun of and laughed at. Therefore, I waited and waited, and with each passing year, Jackie Dee blossomed into a more beautiful young girl than she'd been the year before, to where I thought, "Oh ... my ... God!"

In June of 1974, Jackie and a friend of hers were watching me play football in the street with some friends of mine. By this time, I had let my hair grow to about shoulder length, and I parted it on the side in those days—ah, the seventies. After the game, Jackie and her friend approached me and struck up a conversation with me. We made jokes, laughed, and actually spent a couple of hours together just hanging out and kidding around. It was a day she probably wouldn't remember, but it was a day I will never forget. With each glance, I took of her facial features and expressions. Each word she spoke only confirmed what I was feeling in my heart for her. And that was the fact that I had no doubt she was the one with whom I wanted to spend my life—the girl of my dreams. So, keeping my emotions in check—I waited.

One night when I was about sixteen, I was at a party where adult beverages were being served. I had already tried drinking beer, and I had even tried smoking grass not long before this party. It took some time for me to acquire a taste for beer because I thought it tasted awful, but I soon got used to it. Smoking grass, however, seemed to have an adverse effect on me—it made me irritable, agitated, and apt to become violent, whereas it just seemed to mellow everyone else out.

Anyway, I had a few beers at this party as the night wore on. As the party began to thin out to a small crowd, I began to snuggle up close to the stereo. I was listening through the headphones to Al Green singing "*I'm Still in Love with You*," when I began to inadvertently sing Jackie's name along with the lyrics at a low pitch. Unbeknownst to me, some of the people at the party overheard me singing. They crept up behind me so they could try to hear whose name I was singing, and they heard me singing Jackie's name over and over again. Just then, one of them pulled the headphones off of me and asked so loudly that everyone at the party could hear, "Who is Jackie?"

My best friend, whose name was John and whom I had known since the second grade, was also at the party. John heard all the commotion and asked, "What name did you say?"

They said, "Daniel was singing the name Jackie."

John replied, "Jackie, that's that little girl that lives on his street."

They all laughed at me, and so I told them all to go to hell! I told them they wouldn't understand. Hell, no one would understand, because even I couldn't comprehend how I could feel so strongly about her or why this was happening to me now rather than when we were both older.

Well, as far as that crowd was concerned, my well-guarded secret had been revealed.

I was not ashamed for feeling like I did about Jackie Dee, even though she was so young; I stayed strong at heart and held onto my dream. I stayed up all night that night and part of the next morning thinking about Jackie—her smile, being near her and my vision of us together.

Early the next morning, I thought I had better head for home and get some rest. As I was walking home, I turned the corner onto my street, and I could see Jackie standing in the doorway of the house that was situated there on the corner. I thought, am I dreaming or hallucinating or what? Is she real? When Jackie saw me walking, she waved me over with her hand, so I went over to where she was to say hello. Jackie was standing there smoking a cigarette, and she told me she was babysitting for the people who lived there. She invited me inside and told me to have a seat. Then she asked me if I would like a glass of tea or something, so I said, "Sure, why not."

I watched Jackie move about the place, making me tea and tidying up, with more than just a passing interest. I was completely hypnotized by her every movement and her every word. Jackie and I sat and visited with each other for about an hour and a half, just making idle chatter, drinking tea, and smoking cigarettes. I wanted so much to impress her and gain her approval in some small way, but my mind was not running on all its cylinders after partying the night before. I wanted for the life of me to say something—anything—to Jackie about my feelings for her, but I could not overcome my own shyness or my fear of being rejected. Besides, I did not want to spook her or run her off by coming on to her at this stage of our relationship, which was slowly progressing along. Besides, considering our age difference, there was no way in hell I would have ever said or done anything anyway, even if I hadn't been too damn shy.

After visiting with Jackie for a while, I told her I had better get on home and that I hoped to see her again soon. Of course, what I really wanted to say was, "Jackie, I'm so in love with you that I can't think about anything else, and you are the most beautiful girl I have ever seen, and would you mind spending the rest of your life with me?"

But I just said good-bye and headed for home.

I still felt the need to wait until the right time to make my feelings known to her, but I soon began to observe something that I had not counted on—competition. Now I on occasion, would have girls follow me home from school, and sometimes girls in the neighborhood would come to the house and try to get my attention. Of course, none of them could even turn my head, let alone hold my attention, because I had already been won over by Little Miss Jackie Dee, the girl of my dreams.

However, during 1974 and 1975, a steady stream of boys started hanging around Jackie. You see, Jackie was just as beautiful on the inside as she was on the outside, and it did not take long for anyone to figure this out once they met her. She just had certain qualities about her that pulled you right in. In addition to being so likeable, she was also a very kind and caring person. Jackie Dee was very high-spirited and affectionate in a genuine way, and she was just a pleasant person to be around. The odd thing was that it never caught up to her; even in light of her attractive looks and her many other attributes, she never came off as stuck-up or arrogant. To the contrary, she was extremely modest.

On top of all this, Jackie was physically gifted—she could out-run all the boys on the block, and she was an excellent swimmer. She could also whistle louder than any of us boys could; in fact, Jackie could whistle so loudly that you thought your eardrums were going to burst.

Although there were many guys who were constantly making moves on Jackie, two of them were best friends of mine: Mike and Billy. Billy was my age, and Mike was a little older than I was.

Now, how was I supposed to react to this competition? I felt the need to make my feelings known to her, but I also still felt the need to wait until she was older. Even though Jackie looked much older and acted far more mature than others her age, she was still only twelve years old.

I just couldn't believe it, and if I hadn't known for a fact how old she was, I would have asked to see her birth certificate.

For what ever the reason, I knew that relationships often started at early ages back in the sixties and seventies, when America's culture was in transition, the Vietnam War was going on, and free love and drug abuse was just about everyone's pre-occupation. Our neighborhood was no exception, and relationships sometimes started very early, so none of this was an uncommon occurrence. And God forgive me, but I was not going to stand by and take the chance of losing Jackie to another boy because of some moral inclination of mine. After all, this was the girl of my dreams, and so I reacted the only way I knew how to respond in those days—with lefts and rights. I went after those guys.

The problem was that Jackie was honestly attracted to them. The first time I saw her sitting on Billy's lap, I told him to get his damn hands off her even though he was a friend of mine. Then I proceeded to break them up by yanking Billy out from underneath her, throwing him off his front porch, and tossing him around his front yard like a rag doll. From that point on, I would punch Billy and knock him around in her presence at every opportunity, hoping to impress her and score some points with her. However, I only succeeded in coming off as a bully, even though Billy was taller and outweighed me.

One summer night, I went to the drive-in with Jackie, Billy (whom Jackie did honestly like at the time), and Billy's cousin Lisa. Bob, Lisa's father, was acting as our chaperone. That evening started out as a dream-killer; no matter what I did to get close to Jackie or sit next to her, she would always walk past me and sit next to Billy. The connection between Jackie and me just wasn't apparent to her like it was to me, but why? It was becoming painfully obvious to me that I ignited no fire, or even a spark of emotion in Jackie's heart; God bless her. However, in the meantime, I was always on *fire* for want of her gentle touch, time, and attention.

Not long after that disastrous night, Billy and I were at Jackie's house, and Jackie's mother needed to run a couple of errands. She asked me if I would keep an eye on Jackie and her sister.

I responded, "Keep an eye on Jackie? Sure, I would be more than happy to." All of a sudden, I felt very special, being given such a big responsibility. I was not going to allow anything or anyone to screw it up.

Billy and Jackie kept trying to wander off together, and they were getting a little too close to each other for my liking. When I noticed what was happening right before my very eyes, I became jealous and upset. To the degree that I started knocking Billy around a bit. Finally, his head ricocheted off one of the walls, and he got a headache and went home.

At last, Jackie and I were alone with her little sister. It was so difficult sitting there next to Jackie, talking to her about every-thing except what I really wanted to say to her, that my heart began to beat faster and faster; I could not slow it down. I swear

I was about to burst for wanting to say something—anything—but I just could not for the life of me break down that barrier inside of me and come out with it. It was just killing me not to be able to express what I was feeling for her. The fact that I was worried about our age difference was not helping me either, but guys my age and older came on to Jackie all the time.

I guess I was most fearful of being rejected by her. For some time now, I had been doubting my own personal appeal and my self-worth, and the fact that I could not get Jackie to notice me just crippled me. I was turning the heads of quite a few of the neighborhood girls; some of them were younger than I was, some were my age, and some were even older than I was.

However, I could not get Jackie Dee, the girl of my dreams, to turn her head and notice me. She was affectionate and friendly toward all the guys who came after her and seemed to like everyone but me, and it just drove me nuts. But Jackie was always a very affectionate person by nature.

What in the hell was I doing so wrong that I could not get her to notice me? It was as if I were invisible.

Anyway, while I was watching Jackie and her sister that night, I just did not feel that the time was right to say anything about my feelings for her. After all, she liked my friend Billy, not me. It began to get very late, and she wanted to go to bed, but she was worried about being alone in the house with just her sister. I told her not to worry and that I would sit out on her front porch until her mother returned. Jackie said that it was sweet of me to offer to do that, and then she said good night and went to bed.

There was no way in hell I would ever have left her and her sister alone that night anyway. I didn't trust that creep, Billy, whose head I had smacked against the wall earlier. I thought he might try to sneak back up there to the house if I were to leave. When Jackie's mother returned later that evening, I assured her that everything was fine and told her that they were asleep inside. I went on to tell her that I did not feel comfortable leaving Jackie and her sister alone until she came home. Her mom kissed me on the cheek to thank me for a job well done.

I went home and sat on my own front porch until sunrise, smoking cigarettes and pondering the girl of my dreams, with whom I had just spent the evening. While sitting there on my front porch early that morning, I devised a plan to have my dad take Jackie and me to this huge amusement park called Worlds of Fun. I thought I might be able to spend some quality time with her riding the various rides and that maybe I could try to forge a connection with her if we had a great day just hanging out together.

Everything was going as planned until somehow Billy finagled his way into going with us. I think Jackie must have told Billy about it, because I sure as hell didn't.

Just before we left for the amusement park, we were sitting in my dad's car in front of my house, and my dad was adding up how much money he needed to bring. At the park, there were different admission prices depending on your age. My dad began asking everyone in the car how old we were, and when he came around to Jackie, he said, "Son, how old is she?"

I asked my dad, "Well, how old do you think she is, Dad?"

He said, "I don't know, fifteen—no, sixteen."

I said, "You're exactly right, Dad."

I had lied to my dad, for Jackie was only twelve years old, but the point is that even my dad thought she was much older. Jackie had just turned twelve that summer, but she looked and carried herself like someone who was much older. It was kind of scary because she was more mature than I was in almost every way, and I was seventeen years old. Jackie Dee was street-smart and savvy about life in general, and she even smoked cigarettes, which back in those days was a sign of maturity. She always wore her facial makeup very well. She was so very pleasant to be around; she just had this glow about her that pulled you right in.

Anyway, we all went off to Worlds of Fun, and I'll be damned if the same thing didn't happen there at the amusement park that had happened at the drive-in that one awful night. On some of the rides, they would pair us up in twos. Needless to say, I could never get close enough to Jackie to be paired up with her on a ride because she always stayed so close to Billy. All day long, I kept trying, but I was unable to be paired up with Jackie on a single ride that day. They would always pair me up with someone else.

Even though I was happy that Jackie was having a good time and I was thrilled just to be in her company, seeing her ride the various rides with Billy just crushed me. So much for plots and schemes—I just could not get Jackie to notice me no matter what I tried to do. I thought that maybe I was trying too hard, so I decided to back off.

Around this time, I began to doubt my self-worth even more than ever before, and I wondered if maybe there was something wrong with me.

I had always felt that Jackie Dee was one hundred times more beautiful than I could ever be handsome or good-looking. Although I did not give up on my dream, I did start drinking more and more beer to help me cope with my feelings for her. I tried to keep busy by working several jobs, and I worked out by lifting weights to work off some of my frustrations in addition to my usual fighting and brawling about the neighborhood. I had only two passions in my life back in those days—one was Jackie Dee Stone, and the other was working out with weights. These are still my two obsessions to this very day.

It was around this time that Jackie's mother got married, and Jackie and her family moved in right across the street from me. This was terrific—now I did not have to look any farther than out my living room window to see the girl of my dreams. And every time I saw Jackie Dee, my feelings for her were validated by the fact that I could feel my love for her pulsating inside of my heart.

4

When the Dam around the Heart Breaks

Well anyway, as far as Jackie and Billy's relationship was concerned, Jackie ended up catching mononucleosis from Billy, which as far as I knew could only be contracted through kissing—and probably French kissing at that. I guess the day came when Billy tried to take a little more of something from Jackie than she was ready or willing to give, and she parted ways with him. I hardly had a chance to spit, and before it could even hit the ground, she was already on to contestant number two. I couldn't believe it, no sooner had she gotten away from Billy, she then started seeing another close friend of mine, Mike, the one who was older than I was. So I thought to myself, that's it—this is where I get mean and nasty.

I would sometimes see Jackie and Mike sitting on this little retaining wall out in front of where she used to live or sitting together on her front steps. To this day, I still have a picture that Jackie's mother took of her sitting on Mike's lap on her front steps.

One Saturday evening in the summer of 1975, I had just gotten off work and was sitting out on my front porch, knocking down a couple of cold beers to help me relax. Jackie, it just so happened, was spending the night with one of her girl friends whose family she babysat for from time to time. Jackie's friend lived on the corner of Chelsea Street. My front porch sat up high enough that you could overlook just about every house on the block, and I could see Jackie Dee and Mike out in the front yard of that house.

I swear, every time I saw Jackie Dee, I thought my heart was going to beat right out of my chest. If I was ever going to overcome my shyness and let Jackie Dee know that I was interested in her, and I mean really interested in her, I felt that now was the time. Otherwise, maybe it would all be too late, especially since she had guys lining up at her door.

I had another beer to try to help slow my heart rate down. Then I jumped over the railing of my front porch and headed down the street to join them. I wasn't there even five minutes before Mike started hanging all over Jackie, and then he began trying to kiss her, but Jackie was not responding to his advances. On the contrary, she was clearly trying to shy away from him, and something inside of me just snapped. I put my left hand on Mike's shoulder and jerked him around to face me, away from Jackie. Then I slugged him on the left side of his face with an overhand right. He staggered back, holding his jaw in his hand, and when I drew back to punch him again, he looked at me, then took off and ran away. Mike must have seen this crazy, angered look on my face that I couldn't keep from displaying. I did not give chase because Mike could run extremely fast and I knew I'd never be able to catch him.

I turned to look at Jackie with tears in my eyes. She was puzzled, to say the least, by what I had just done. Unable to control my desire for her after all this time, I threw my arms around her shoulders and gazed into those beautiful, hazel-colored eyes of hers. When Jackie looked back into my eyes, I began kissing her on the lips. When my lips touched hers for the very first time, something wonderful began to happen inside of me. It was like heaven—or what heaven ought to be like. This first kiss was fascinating, much like that first smile that had left me hypnotized and spellbound. And from that night on, any time I held Jackie in my arms and her lips touched mine, it was like some sort of awareness settled on my heart and mind, reassuring me that we were really meant to be together.

I could only assume that Jackie was feeling the same way, because she in no way resisted my advances. Instead, she responded to me in a most affectionate manner. And on that night, as I held Jackie Dee in my arms, I stopped kissing her for a moment and began telling her just how I felt about her.

I remember telling Jackie how much I loved her and how incredibly wonderful it felt to finally hold her close to me. I told Jackie that she had no idea how long I had been waiting to share this one very special moment with her—the moment when we would kiss each other for the very first time.

Upon hearing all of this, Jackie Dee was receptive to my advances to say the least. She began to tell me about her own emotions and feelings that—amazingly enough—she had been holding back for me! She told me that she was very fond of me as well, which was like beautiful music to my ears. Then she slipped her arms around me, holding me every bit as tight and as close as I was already holding her, and began kissing me on the lips again.

Up until that point in my life, I had never been kissed or held as she was kissing and holding me—yikes! I'd had numerous pecks on the cheek or lips, but there had been nothing like this, where it meant so much to me. When Jackie began kissing me, for the first time—I could feel passionate, pleasurable emotions controlling my every movement.

I can remember, up until that night anyway, it was like a dam had been placed around my heart that had been keeping me from expressing my feelings and emotions to Jackie. Now I could feel the dam beginning to break apart and letting everything I was feeling for her on the inside flow outward!

I had heard and read about what paradise was supposed to be like, but as far as I was concerned, paradise was just holding Jackie Dee in my arms, loving her ever so tenderly and affectionately. I did not want to let go of her all night. I did not want that night ever to end. With each embrace, with each time her long, honey-blonde hair brushed against my face and neck, with each kiss of her lips, I found another facet of paradise. The fragrance that emanated from her soft skin flowed into my nostrils, and as it made its way to my heart, I became so dizzy that I thought I was going to pass out right there in Jackie Dee's arms. My heart was beating so fast and felt so out of control that I simply could not slow it down.

Well having survived that magic moment, Jackie and I ended up lying on top of a table that was situated in the front yard of the house where she was spending the night, and we continued making out all night. I was finally kissing the beautiful face of the little girl who had displayed that lethal smile that had swept me away so long ago.

All that night, I did not want Jackie to stray too far from me. If she did get out of arm's reach, I would say, "Come here, come here." All that night, it seemed like I was saying, "Come here." Jackie was doing this on purpose, you see, because she wanted to hear me call to her over and over again.

As the night continued to slip away, we ended up sitting out on the front sidewalk kissing one another, smoking cigarettes, and drinking some of my dad's Schlitz beer until daybreak. Yes, I saw fireworks that night. I saw the sky parting like a scroll. And yes, the cows even came home. Yes, I know she was only twelve, but none of that mattered now, now that I had finally made some of my feelings known to her.

Once again, Jackie was not your typical twelve-year-old girl. She was uncannily mature, street-wise, and smart for her age. She was attending modeling school, and because she was mature beyond her years, she'd had grown men from all around the neighborhood making advances at her for well over a year now. Even male friends of her mother and her aunt's were coming on to her. At the age of nine, the flower of her womanhood had begun to blossom, and I could go on—believe me. Jackie was undoubtedly years ahead of the curve on all levels from a maturity standpoint—wow!

As for me, this one very special night with Jackie Dee, so full of purity and innocence, was the best day of my life. I have no problem admitting that this particular night with her was a monumental event for me, especially considering everything that I had experienced since I had first seen her smile on that most memorable day. God forgive me, but I was not going to be cheated on that night by second-guessing myself morally, spiritually, or in any other way.

The night was shaping up to be a dream come true. I had such a wonderful time with Jackie Dee, the girl of my dreams, on this night that I felt like I could leap from a high-flying airplane and hit the ground running.

I honestly felt that if I had waited any longer, I might never have gotten another chance to make my feelings known to her, so I felt I had to make a move right then. Is there anyone out there who can possibly understand this? Is there anyone out there this side of sanity who can relate to what was happening inside of me or see why I felt it was time to do something about it? If I hadn't had a few drinks that night, I would probably still be sitting on my front porch, waiting for the right moment to make my move ...

Here's the pay-off, and to think that the love Jackie and I exchanged on that night, the heights of human emotion we attained, took place without any sex involved! It was one of the most erotic, sensual, and passionate encounters I can ever remember having. I can remember almost every detail of that night as if it were yesterday even though it took place more than thirty years ago. I remember the beating of our hearts, riveting and pulsating together as one heartbeat as we held each other so very close and tight. It was truly one of the most memorable evenings I've ever experienced, filled with so many precious moments. Precious moments like when I would reach out to Jackie—to hold her hand in mine, or the way the moonlight danced in her eyes, and when I would brush her hair back away from her cheeks with my fingers each time I kissed her. In the end, it was a night that I will never forget. It was just that incredible.

You know, there is nothing like being genuinely in love and feeling the excitement it brings to you. I'm talking about loving someone truly, deeply, and madly, the way I was and still am in love with Jackie Dee. It permeates every aspect of your life to the point at which you cannot think about anything else.

Sex, on the other hand, was something with which I was entirely unfamiliar at the time. Before that night, I had never put myself in a position where I could learn about it or be tempted into doing something that I had no interest in doing. Besides, I was always too busy fighting and getting into trouble. All my friends were sexually active, or so they said, but not me. I was keeping myself for one person and one person only—the girl of my dreams—with a hope and a prayer that maybe she would be willing to do the same for me.

On that first night with Jackie, I simply was not mature enough to make love to her, nor was she ready. Believe me; I would not even have known what to do in the first place. I was completely oblivious of what to put where and so forth.

Somewhere in the midst of our loving each other that night, it seemed that something kept reassuring my heart and mind over and over again. It told me that there was still so very much more love for the two of us to exchange throughout the rest of our lives. Moreover, it told me that we really hadn't even scratched the surface of what each of us had in store for the other. To put it another way, we hadn't seen or experienced anything yet; as far as the breadth, length, depth, and height of how infinite and far reaching this love of ours could take us. As good as it was for Jackie Dee and I on that night, the best was yet to come.

All that night, we made out, conversed, drank beer, and smoked cigarettes until the break of day. This very special night with Jackie that I did not want to ever end, was rapidly dissipating as the sunlight crept over the horizon and began to chase the remnants of the night away. In the wee hours of the morning, Jackie and I made plans to meet up at Cool Crest swimming pool later that day. We then began to say our good-byes with hugs and kisses.

As I began to cross the street and head for home, I turned around and walked backwards so that I could keep looking back at Jackie for that one last look of her standing there. She stood there smiling at me so enticingly that I began blowing kisses at her. Then I stopped, made my way back across the street to her, and held her in my arms for one last kiss.

I probably did this four or five times until finally I had to give it up and head home for real; it was now daylight out, and the neighborhood was beginning to wake up.

Thank you ever so much, Jackie Dee, for that wondrous night when you touched not only my heart but my very soul. I will remember it always.

Once I made it back home and into my bed, I remember not being able to sleep. Even though my mind and body needed rest, my heart just wouldn't let go of what had taken place just minutes and hours before.

As I lay there in my bed that morning, I kept thinking that Jackie Dee had probably never seen any of this coming in her wildest dreams, but I had. I mean, my punching my friend in the face, running him off so that I could come on to her, and launching myself at her the way I did was inevitable. After all, this was the girl of my dreams, Miss Jackie Dee Stone. I'm sure Jackie had never in her life been showered with such a barrage of love and affection as I had unleashed on her that night. It was definitely a new experience for me as well, loving someone to the extent that I had loved her on that very special night. I could hardly believe I had finally breached the barrier of my own inhibitions and shyness—I had finally succeeded in taking Jackie in my arms and kissing her like I had wanted to do since that first day I'd seen her smile.

I wanted so very much to believe that our first kiss had ignited the fires of passion in Jackie Dee like her smile had ignited my passion for her, but had it? If it had, then the trick would be to carry that fire without burning each other like I had seen other couples do before.

Amazingly enough, I can still recall the intense anxiety I felt when I anticipated seeing her again. I mean, I knew it was only a few hours before I would see Jackie at Cool Crest, but that was too long of a wait, as far as I was concerned. I wondered how she would act towards me, considering everything that had taken place the night before.

That Sunday afternoon, we met up at the swimming pool. When I saw Jackie Dee in her white, two-piece bathing suit walking toward me with that darling smile of hers, I literally just gasped. My jaw dropped open and hit the deck—yikes! Jackie Dee was simply drop-dead gorgeous; there is no other way to describe her. I can remember seeing on the top and bottom portion of Jackie's swimsuit, she had a little heart shape cut out of the material that would leave a little heart shape tan on her breast, as well as on her behind, if you know what I mean. I was totally unprepared to see her in a bathing suit that day. I mean, I suspected all along that she had the shape and figure to go with everything else that was attractive and adorable about her, but somehow, I was still not prepared. What was I thinking? I had no idea that she would look so damn good! Jackie Dee was just absolutely breathtaking, and to think that she was only twelve years old!

Anyway, she definitely got my heart rate, my adrenaline, my hormones, and you name it elevated that day. You couldn't have slowed my heart down with Thorazine. After all these years, I can still see Jackie on that day at the swimming pool in my mind's eye, and it still makes me shake all over.

I spent the whole day at her elbow, warding off anyone who tried to get too close to us. She was an excellent swimmer and diver, so I had to work extra hard to keep up with her. We did not exactly pick up where we left off the night before; this was partially because I had not had any alcohol and partially because we were now in the company of just about every kid who lived on our block. They were all watching us, wondering what was going on between us because we were hanging out so close to one another and trying to keep away from everybody so we could be alone. We were quite the talk of the neighborhood from then on.

That day at the pool, Jackie Dee could have done whatever she wanted to do to me, and I would have willingly let her. It was like I was her puppet for a day.

From that day forth, we tried to see each other as much as we possibly could.

Jackie and I also spent a lot of time talking on the telephone when it was not possible for us to see each other for one reason or another. Most of the time we did spend together took place on my front porch or somewhere in front of our houses, where her mom and step-dad could keep a watchful eye on us.

One day in August, Jackie and I were standing very close to one another on my front porch and leaning against the porch railing. She was wearing these tight, bell-bottom blue jeans and a button-down, collared, denim shirt. Her facial make-up was perfect, and her long, honey-blonde hair was attractively arranged. Her top was unbuttoned about halfway, and she was talking about how we should get together over at her aunt's house later that night. I wanted to take Jackie in my arms and kiss her so badly, and I could sense that she wanted to kiss me as well.

However, we both knew that we were being watched—we could feel her folks' and our neighbor's eyes upon us. In the end, we knew that it would just cause us problems if we were to kiss each other openly right there—in that moment. How extremely frustrating it was for the two of us!

As I stood there looking at her, I could see a glow around her that was similar to what I had seen when I first saw her smile from across the street years earlier. And as if that wasn't enough, every time I was around Jackie Dee, I could detect this seductive body fragrance coming from her. It had an ambrosial, intoxicating effect on me that would leave me breathless and dizzy.

Standing there on my front porch that day, Jackie truly was a vision of beauty to behold, and it left a lasting impression on my heart and mind. I thought my God in heaven, Jackie Dee couldn't have been any more beautiful than she was on that day—or could she? I can still remember seeing her standing there, leaning against the porch rail, to this very day.

Jackie's aunt would sometimes allow the two of us to see each other at her place, or sometimes I would go see Jackie when she was babysitting in the neighborhood. That night, Jackie and I got together over at her aunt's house after I'd had a few drinks at a friend's house that lived about a block away. We sat out on the front steps side-by-side, surrounded by the stars that filled the night sky above us, talking about how good it felt to be so close and near each other again. I was so uncontrollably drawn to Jackie that I was absolutely bursting at the seams with the desire to take her in my arms and hold her ever so close to me. I remember putting my arm around Jackie's shoulder, and before long we were all over each other, making out in front of her aunt's house. Later that night, we ended up in her aunt's car, which was parked in the driveway. We spent all night getting close, intimate, and affectionate with each other. As the night began to give way to the light of day, we had to say our good-byes, as hard as it was for us, not knowing when we would be able to see each other again; at least where we could be alone anyway. With tears in my eyes and an aching heart, I finally let go from holding her in my arms. This would be the second time that Jackie and I had spent the entire night—together.

We came close that night and early that next morning to doing more than just hugging and kissing each other; our hands just seemed to find their way here and there, but I did not know what to do next. What probably came naturally to other guys did not come naturally to me.

I remember that when I did get to see Jackie Dee when I was sober, I could never muster enough courage to plant a kiss squarely on her lips. Because of this, every time we had to say good-bye, I would tell Jackie, "You owe me one."

She would reply, "I owe you one of what?"

However, I would not tell her what it was that she owed me during this time span we were unable to be completely alone with each other. I kept this up day in and day out, telling Jackie that she owed me one, and soon the number of things she owed me began to get pretty large—like twenty-six or something.

Finally, I thought I had better tell her what it was that she owed me.

It was simply a kiss for every time we had to say good-bye after visiting each other—since we could not openly kiss in public—on our street anyway. The reason for this was that we thought that if her folks saw us being affectionate toward one another or if they heard about it from one of our nosy neighbors, her parents would more than likely not allow Jackie to see me anymore. Nevertheless, Jackie Dee—my sweetheart—affectionately paid me in full with all those kisses she owed me.

In spite of all of our precautions and our efforts to hide how we really felt about each other, Jackie's parents were already trying to discourage her from seeing me for a variety of reasons. One was that they felt that Jackie was too young to be seeing anybody, and they were right. Two, they were fearful of Jackie Dee becoming pregnant by me, even though they didn't know that sex was the furthest thing from my heart and mind. Three, my reputation around the neighborhood did not exactly portray the kind of character any parent would want their daughter to be associated with. Four, I was five years older than Jackie was.

It was around this time when Jackie and I were struggling to find ways to see each other that my father was diagnosed with terminal cancer. It was January of 1976, and I was seventeen at the time. Even though I was not close to my dad, the thought of losing him was just impossible for me to accept. I remember that my mind seemed to be in a fog a lot of the time during that period of my life.

That year, I watched my father die the sort of slow, torturous death that's usually associated with the effects of cancer, and there was nothing I could do to ease his pain. Just the very thought of not being able to ask my dad for advice or not seeing him sitting in his favorite chair when I walked through our living room was simply unbearable. I began to drink more beer, get into more fights, and of course, get into more trouble. My hair was now parted down the middle, and it went halfway down my back.

It was also around this time that I started carrying a handgun. One of the reasons for this was that I had received some threats for defending and protecting some friends of mine in a car deal that had gone bad. Another reason was that one evening in March, my friend Billy and I were wrestling on the corner of my street to work off some steam just horsing around. Just then, a 1972 or 1973, bluish-green Chevy Impala drove up alongside us. A man inside the car yelled at us to come over to the car. In response, I gave him the ever-so-popular hand gesture I liked to use in those days, but the man continued to yell at us to come near the vehicle. I just ignored him and continued wrestling with Billy. There were probably three or more people in the vehicle yelling at us, but they finally seemed to give up and drove away down 24th Street.

A few minutes later, Billy and I heard a popping sound coming from the direction the car had just headed. Within minutes, we heard emergency vehicles racing toward that spot, so Billy and I headed in that direction. Apparently, some friends of ours had been sitting on a wall on the corner, across the street from a soda fountain shop. The same people that had pulled up alongside us just minutes before had driven up to these friends of ours and yelled at them to come over to the car. As two of our friends approached the vehicle, someone sitting in the back seat opened fired on them with a shotgun, killing one of them and seriously injuring the other before speeding away. To my knowledge, the shooters were never captured.

Needless to say, it could just as easily have been Billy or me who was fired upon or killed that night had we stopped wrestling and approached the vehicle. Because of that incident and due to the fact that the neighborhood was becoming increasingly unstable, I started carrying a handgun with me most of the time.

Early in the spring, when the passing of my father was quickly approaching, I think Jackie's mom began to feel a little sorry for me. There were a couple of times that her mother let me visit with Jackie Dee on her front porch when it was very late, even though I think her mom knew I had been drinking.

Then Jackie and I would wander over to the driveway of her next-door neighbor's house and sit on this little, white wall behind the bushes. Once we had hidden ourselves back there, we would hold and kiss each other and really just enjoy each other's company.

I did not have any problems kissing Jackie or expressing how I felt about her while I was under the influence of adult beverages—it all just came out. It is sad to say, though, that that was the only time I could express to Jackie what I was feeling for her, and to comfortably take her into my arms and kiss her. I just could not overcome my inhibitions and shyness. I honestly felt like I was being restrained by some kind of force that kept me from expressing myself when I was sober. It just wasn't fair—I could walk up and punch anyone right in the face, but I could not walk up and kiss the girl of my dreams, even though by that point in time we were quite emotionally involved with each other.

On Saturday, April 17 of 1976, I turned eighteen years old. For my birthday, Jackie gave me the *Peter Frampton Comes Alive* double album that was hot off the press. Jackie wanted to give me the present before leaving for her grandma's farm in Stover, Missouri, or what I referred to as "the funny farm" in those days. We were standing out on the sidewalk in front of my house when she gave it to me, and to show my appreciation, I embraced her. Then I planted a big, wet, sloppy kiss on her lips in broad daylight, right out in plain view for everyone to see. In turn, Jackie Dee gave me a big, wet, sloppy birthday kiss, which to this day is the best birthday present I have ever received.

It felt great to hold Jackie in my arms and kiss her out in public like that. I felt like a tremendous weight was lifted off my shoulders. After Jackie and I had exchanged those birthday kisses, we began to pick our spots and kiss each other in public more openly and more often now.

That night, I went to the drive-in with my friends Billy and Pat. I was drinking rather heavily that night, and everything seemed to be going okay. Billy and Pat, as it turned out, were trying to come on to these girls at the concession stand—one of which was a real looker, or so I was told. I was back at the car, watching the movie and waiting for them to return with some things to snack on.

Little did Billy or Pat know that these girls were there with their boyfriends, who were not around at the time Billy and Pat were busy trying to make a move on them. Apparently, these girls did not tell Billy or Pat that they were at the drive-in with somebody else. To make matters worse, these girls baited them back to their vehicles they and there boyfriends were driving that night. They were also there with some friends of theirs who were in another car.

When Billy and Pat followed these girls back to their vehicles, some guys jumped out of several cars and started giving them a hard time. They accused Billy and Pat of trying to steal their girlfriends from them. They started pushing my friends around, and then they began punching them with their fists. Billy and Pat took off running across the drive-in parking lot, trying to get away from these guys. I saw them come running up to our car, so I got out to see what was wrong. Billy and Pat were so scared that they practically knocked me down as I was getting out of the car. I could not make out what they were yelling as they climbed into the car, closing the doors behind them.

Just then, the guys that were chasing my friends came running up to the car and started yelling at me.

I dropped the first guy who put his hand on me like a sack of potatoes with an overhand right to the left side of his face. I hollered for Pat and Billy to get out of the car and help me, but they didn't. Instead, they locked the car doors. Now, I had suspected that Billy had a yellow streak in him, but not Pat. I'd always thought he was made of sterner stuff.

After I had dropped this first clown, I jumped backward, rolling over the trunk of the car and landing on my feet with my fists cocked, putting a little distance between them and me. There were too many of them, though, and they were all over me. I thought I was doing a pretty good job of holding my own, but then I was hit with a car jack right in the middle of my back. As I started to go down, I lunged at one of the guys who was landing some pretty good shots on me.

I grabbed him around his waist, and down we both went. I worked my left arm up around his neck in a headlock position and began choking him.

The other guys in his company began kicking me and pulling my long hair. They were trying to pull me off of him, but I would not let go. I tried to slide myself up under the back of the car for some cover from the kicking and punching, dragging him along with me. Then I took my thumb and drove it into his left eye. I drove it in with such force that blood began squirting down my arm and chest. The more he fought and tried to wrestle away from me, the deeper I drove my thumb into his eye. He was screaming bloody murder. To this day, I have never heard anyone scream like he did on that night. The other guys finally broke my hold on him and dragged him away from me.

Finally, some drive-in attendants came and broke the whole thing up. Just before the attendants showed up, though, I was thinking long and hard about using the knife or even the gun I was carrying. But everything happened so fast that it was over just as quickly as it had started.

Before that night, I had made a personal vow to myself never to use the gun or the knife in a fistfight—I would only use them if I found myself or someone else in a life-threatening situation. Then I would not hesitate to use them.

The drive-in attendants asked us if either party wanted to get the police involved, press charges or whatever. I responded, "Absolutely not." The other party did not want the police involved either.

The attendants told us that if they heard so much as a peep out of either party again, they were going to call the police, and then they left. From the first punch I had thrown to when the attendants broke up the fight, it was all over in less than a couple of minutes.

There were locks of hair ripped out of my head and a cut over my left eye. I could not hear a thing out of my left ear, and I had a huge welt in the middle of my back. I had sustained several gashes to my left arm and knee to go along with the drive-in gravel that was embedded in my left elbow. I could not find my left shoe, and I had lost my thumb-ring in that guy's eye socket.

As I lit up a cigarette, Billy and Pat finally saw that the guys had retreated to their vehicles and got out of the car. I yelled at my friends, calling them cowards and pansies as well as a few other choice names. Then I dowsed my cigarette out on Pat's forehead and punched him in the face, but they both took off and ran away from me. I took off my right shoe and threw it at them as they ran off across the parking lot.

I waited for them to return to the car for a little bit. When they didn't come back, I became so enraged by their refusal to get off their asses and help me that I torched Pat's car. I set it on fire by using some lighter fluid that I found under the seat.

As I was walking home that night, I could see the flames coming from the car from quite far away. I remember thinking what a terrific eighteenth birthday this night had turned out to be as I tried to dig the pieces of gravel out of my elbow. I walked all the way home from the drive-in bruised, battered, and barefoot that night. I never did find out why these guys were chasing Billy and Pat—that night. I would have to wait for another day to find out how it all got started. Needless to say, it was a long time before I spoke to either one of those chicken-shits Billy and Pat again.

It was now early in the month of July, and I was feeling really down about my father's imminent death literally just days away. I was also upset that I had not been able to see or even talk to Jackie Dee for more than a week for various reasons. Mostly though, because her parents were beginning to limit when Jackie could leave the house to see me or even talk to me over the telephone.

On one particular night, I was sitting on my front porch when a myriad of life's uncertainties flooded my mind. However, these thoughts were quickly overshadowed by my strong desire to see Jackie Dee, if only for a brief moment. But how could I possibly see her when it was so late and I was sure that she was asleep in the comfort of her own bed?

Nevertheless, I kept hoping, wishing, and praying that I might somehow get to see her that night. Just seeing Jackie Dee or hearing the sound of her voice would give me the courage and strength that I so desperately needed to cope with everything that was falling apart around me. I needed to see her right then more than I ever had before. I must have sat there on my front porch for hours just thinking of her. It began to get very late.

Around two o'clock in the morning, as I sat there gazing across the street at her house and missing her, lo and behold, I saw the front door of her house begin to open. You are not going to believe this, but it was none other than Jackie Dee, coming out of her house ever so quietly. I sat there in utter shock and amazement; I just could not believe it. It was as if I had willed her to come out of her house, and there she was. For a moment, I could not move or speak, but only for a moment. Then I jumped to my feet, leaped over the handrail, jumped off the garage and onto the sidewalk below, hit the ground running, and raced across the street.

As Jackie saw me making my way toward her, she began shushing me to keep quiet and to calm down. I rushed over to her, and she stood there waiting for me on her front porch. Like some kind of scene out of Romeo and Juliet, we embraced and then began kissing each other ever so passionately that I'm sure if anyone would have been awake to witness it, would have thought, "This couple must really be in love—wow!"

Jackie tried in vain to calm me down; I was so excited to see her and hold her in my arms once again. We spoke only in whispers so as not to be heard by anyone. I started kissing Jackie on her lips, face, and neck, and I was so happy to be holding her in my arms once again—and without the aid of any alcohol or drugs, I might add. It was just passion, pure as the driven snow that was controlling my every move.

I asked Jackie rather excitedly, "What are you doing out here so late?"

She said, "I'm not really sure why I came outside. Something woke me up, and I felt compelled to just get up out of bed and come outside."

Jackie said she had looked out the window and thought she could see me sitting out on my front porch. She said, "I thought that since I was going outside anyway, I might as well grab my cigarettes and have a smoke."

I said, "Thank you, thank you, thank you for hearing my heart's cry; in my heart, I was calling out your name and hoping, wishing, and praying that you would hear me and listen, and—you did it!"

Jackie and I held each other right there on her front porch, doing everything possible to make every second count twice. We used this time to get close and intimate with each other as we continued to speak in whispers for the next hour or so. Finally, Jackie decided she had better head back inside before her parents noticed that she was not in her bed.

I told Jackie that God was going to have to help me let go from holding her because I knew that I would not be able to do it on my own. Jackie reassured me that I would see her again later that afternoon, but I knew there was a strong possibility that that would not happen. Since her parents were restricting her so much now, the times we did get to see each other were sporadic at best.

Finally, I let go of her after placing one last kiss on her lips. As she turned to go, Jackie passed me a hand-written note and asked me to read it when I got back home. I watched her go back inside the house as I started to back away from her front steps, hoping to see her smile at me one last time. Once she was back inside the house, I could see her smiling and waving good-bye to me through the screen door. I blew her a kiss and thought that now I could finally get some sleep.

Elated, excited, and feeling somewhat beside myself, I seemed to float across the street. I headed for the back door of my house and crawled into my bed. Then I pulled Jackie's note out of my pocket and began reading it. Something immediately jumped right off the page and caught my eye.

Jackie stated in her note that she without a doubt wanted me to be her *first*. That is, the first one to make love to her when she felt that she was ready and the time was right.

This letter was only one in a series of notes that Jackie would write me that summer promising me this unbelievable treasure. These notes not only confirmed what I had believed all along about the two of us but also affirmed that everything was falling into place.

To say the least, I felt so honored that Jackie would want to bestow this—what I considered a gift from God—on me. Even though making love to Jackie was the furthest thing from my mind at the time, I was still touched, moved, and filled with sweet emotions by her promise. This was something I was hopeful her and I could explore together when the right time came—being our first time and all. My plan was to wait, possibly even until we were married—that is, if I could convince Jackie to wait until then.

As I lay there drifting off to sleep, I felt that God had performed a miracle by allowing me to see the girl of my dreams—once again. However, even more importantly concerning that night was Jackie's note. Her note was by far the greatest promise anyone had ever made to me in my entire life, and what an incredibly pleasant surprise that was. Thank you, God.

5

Paradise Lost!
(Peace and Tranquility
among the Tombs)

As I previously mentioned, Jackie's parents were trying to pull the plug on our relationship and split us up with threats directed at me. And who could blame them, really? They were just looking out for what was in the best interest of their daughter, and that clearly didn't include me. After all, she was only twelve years old, soon to be thirteen that July, and I had just turned eighteen. Jackie's parents also knew that my brothers and I had had some scrapes with the law. Nothing serious, mind you, just misdemeanors like fighting and brawling about in public. And that we were a somewhat unruly bunch, and we were poor.

Two weeks after Jackie turned thirteen, my father passed away on my mother's forty-seventh birthday: August 4, 1976. It was just after one o'clock in the morning when my mother, sister, brothers, and I watched my dad pass from this life into eternity.

As we committed his body to the ground from which it was formed, the family seemed to fall apart, and we all pretty much went our separate ways. We were never that close to begin with, but now we became even more distant.

Losing my dad was absolutely devastating for me. He was only forty-seven years old when he died. I began to drink beer more often, and I took all kinds of drugs to help me cope with his death and with all the other horrors from my past that were eating away at me inside.

One of my last recollections of holding Jackie in my arms and kissing her that year was shortly after the passing of my father. Jackie and I were sitting in a tan, '67 Pontiac Tempest that was parked in my driveway. My brother had sold the car to me, but it needed some work before it would run again. That night, while Jackie and I were enjoying being close and affectionate with one another, I kind of got the sense that she was ready to take our relationship to the next level. As she was now beginning to indicate this in her letters to me. However, I was not ready to do so for two reasons. The most obvious reason was that Jackie was still too young. The other reason was that I was not ready either, even though I was eighteen years old.

Now, please don't misunderstand me: everything in me worked from a physiological standpoint. I mean, believe me, every time I saw Jackie Dee or heard her voice over the telephone or even thought about her, the usual physiological functions in my mind and my body would react involuntary. It often made me feel most uncomfortable, if you know what I mean. I simply was not ready or willing to have sex with Jackie Dee at that point in time. Besides, as ridiculous as it may sound, I still did not know how to do it. It was unexplored and uncharted territory for me to which I just didn't have a clue and rather preferred it that way, at least for the time being. Nevertheless, Jackie and I had taken our relationship as far as two people in love could go without taking that next step.

Shortly after that night, Jackie's parents stepped up their efforts to keep us apart, and they stopped allowing Jackie to see or call me. We had to resort to passing hand-written notes to one another through a mutual acquaintance of ours and relaying our messages through a courier. On occasion, Jackie would sneak a phone call to me. Jackie and I kept trying to see each other secretly as often as we could, but we could never spend any quality time alone together. The pressure from her parents, friends, and relatives and the fact that she had started seeing someone else at church began to strain our relationship to the point that our break-up seemed inevitable. The days that were just on the horizon for me would be some of the worst days of my entire life.

In October, just two months after the passing of my father, Jackie sent her friend Pamela over one evening to act as our courier. There were rumors going around town that Jackie was seeing someone else, and Pamela was supposed to ask me how I felt about Jackie and whether I still considered her my girlfriend. Of course, these rumors were tearing me apart internally; I did not want to believe they were true, but they were. On the heels of losing my father, it was extremely difficult for me to fight back my tears and give the proper response that would convey how I felt about Jackie Dee. I can remember this encounter as being one of those events in my life when it was most troublesome for me to try to communicate to a third party—and a girl, no less—what I was feeling about the girl of my dreams.

To make matters worse, I was generally somewhat stoic by nature; this was partially because I'd been raised that way and partially because of the things I'd suffered in my youth. I had always internalized everything I was feeling and was not very good at expressing it. I told Pamela to tell Jackie that nothing had changed concerning my feelings for her and that I still loved her and would very much like to continue seeing her. Believe me, it took every ounce of fortitude that I could muster to give even that much of a response. I was so shy and timid, and without the aid of an adult beverage, that was simply the best I could do.

Pamela started criticizing me about Jackie's and my age difference and told me that it was wrong for me to even continue to like Jackie, let alone continue seeing her.

I said, "Hey, I thought Jackie sent you over here to find out how I felt about her, so don't think for one second that you are going to stand here on my front porch and lecture me on this same old age disparity bullshit." And to put it politely, I told Pam to get the hell off my front porch.

That weekend, Jackie called me up on the telephone to tell me that she really liked me but that she had met someone else and was going to start seeing him. Jackie begged me to please, please promise her not to interfere or do anything crazy. She went on to say that it was probably for the best because of our age difference and because of all the opposition we had to deal with from her parents and our neighbors. Jackie also said that the person she'd met went to her church, that his name was Mark, and that he was a born-again Christian.

I thought to myself, "What does that mean? Born again?"

Jackie went on to explain that she was going to start attending church with her mother. She told me that things just weren't working out between us and that it was over.

I promised Jackie that I would not interfere, but I could not promise her that I would not do something crazy. I know this sounds pathetic, but while I still had Jackie on the phone, I truly wanted to beg her with every ounce of emotion I could muster not to break up with me and start seeing someone else. Instead, all I could muster was a faint voice that said, "Please don't do this Jackie—please don't go."

I felt like I'd died right there on my living room floor after she hung up the telephone. This was my darkest hour, the absolute worst day of my stinking life. I began to doubt my self-worth even more than ever before; I was devastated.

As I sat there dwelling on the thought of not having Jackie Dee, the girl of my dreams, as my girlfriend, I became so physically ill that I began throwing up, and then passed out. I lay there in what felt like a comatose state, unable to move a muscle yet aware of everything that was going on around me. Even though I was unable to move, I could feel my heart beating so fast that I thought I was going to have a heart attack right there on my living room floor.

My mind kept rehashing the day's events as well as the other events that had occurred in my life to lead me up to this point. Outside of the one bright spot of my vision of Jackie Dee and I, the times we shared together, and now that she was gone, my life was just a long series of disappointments, one right after the other.

The thought of not being able to look into those hazel-colored eyes of hers, to embrace her, or to kiss those lips that displayed the smile, which captured my heart so long ago was literally crushing the life right out of me. I thought, "This is it; this is how death is going to come to me," as I lay there on my living room floor.

I came to hours later, so very weak and thirsty, but I had survived whatever kind of an attack that was. The loss of Jackie was still heavy on my heart and mind, but I would live to see another day, though I was not sure if I really wanted to. I picked myself up off the floor and began pouring alcohol into my body by the gallons and taking stimulants and depressants at an overdose pace. I realized that I was now back in familiar territory—I was having a one-sided love affair with Jackie Dee again.

One night when I had been drinking quite a bit of alcohol, I just so happened to catch up with this fellow named Mark, whom Jackie was now dating, at a nearby convenience store. As fate would have it, I was carrying my pistol, as I did from time to time. The east side of town where we lived was becoming more unstable with characters like myself running around, so as I mentioned earlier, I carried a gun or knife with me on occasion.

I surprised Mark by opening the passenger door of his vehicle and getting into his car. I said to him, "Let's go for a little drive."

I knew this asshole from school and from around the neighborhood, and he knew who I was too. The alcohol and God only knows what else were influencing me quite a lot that night. I was so full of rage that Mark was now seeing the girl of my dreams that at the moment I had entered his vehicle, I had every intention of killing him.

I was trying to think of a remote area to have him drive to so I could shoot him, and I decided to do it in a nearby park. I told him to drive down Topping Street and into the park. I really didn't need the gun because I could easily have dismembered him with my bare hands. I kept remembering Jackie asking me to please not to interfere, and I was already in jeopardy of invalidating the promise I had made to her by going this far. I was torn and conflicted, and I wrestled with myself about whether or not to shoot him as we drove around.

My thoughts of killing this creep were interrupted when he offered me a beer. Then he surprised me by asking me if I wanted to smoke a joint with him; he had just scored some new stuff from a mutual acquaintance of ours. He lit the joint up and began smoking it as he rambled on rather nervously about all the girlfriends he had at school and church. Then he went on to say that when his grandmother, or aunt or somebody passed away, he would inherit her house and car and blah, blah, blah.

I hardly said anything to Mark as we drove around because I really did not have anything to say to him. I just wanted to put a bullet or two in his face. As for sharing a joint with this asshole, I told him I had better pass. I knew that if I did, he would have no chance whatsoever of surviving the night. I didn't even take the beer he offered me because I wanted nothing from him; then again, I also wanted everything from him in that I wanted to take his life. In all his boasting, he never once uttered Jackie's name or mentioned anything about her.

At one point, I asked Mark in a rather provoking manner if he was finished and did he ever shut the hell up long enough to come up for some damn air. He hardly said anything after that, and we drove around for a little while until I told him to drop me off at the next corner. I had the gun in my right hand, and I kept remembering Jackie begging me to please, please not interfere or do anything crazy.

As I was getting ready to get out of the car, this thought came to me: if you do what you're thinking about doing—which was killing him—it's not going to all of a sudden make Jackie start loving you again, if she ever really did in the first place. Rather, she would probably hate you if she ever found out that you wasted him.

Nevertheless, I know I scared the crap out of Mark. He probably wet his pants that night.

But life was already trying to teach me a valuable lesson, which was that you cannot make someone love you, no matter how hard you try. You just can't do it—it's either there or it's not.

Anyway, I was really confused now, because Mark was supposed to be a Christian, and yet he smoked and drank. So what was the difference between him and me? And in talking to this butthead as we were driving around that night, I found out that Mark was just a few months younger than I was. So how did Jackie's dating him solve the issue of this age disparity bullshit I'd been hearing so damn much about? What was it that made Jackie and her parents think that her going steady with this creep was better than her seeing me?

The difference between Mark and me was that Jackie now liked him, not me. Moreover, he could offer her more than I could from a materialistic standpoint because of what he stood to inherit when his grandmother or somebody died. I guess it all boiled down to some kind of security crap, which to some people means everything, I guess, or so I was told. The only things I could offer Jackie in terms of security were my dreams and a love that was genuine and immeasurable.

At that point in my life, for all intents and purposes, I just needed someone to believe in me and to stand by me. Not only was my heart already breaking from the loss of my father, but I had also just lost paradise and the only dream I'd ever had. I wondered if it would have been better not to have tasted paradise at all instead of having held it in my arms only to lose it to another. But I still would have chosen the latter. Even if I had only gotten to hold Jackie Dee in my arms for a brief moment in time, it would have been worth having my heart ripped out of my chest and suffer the nightmares that would haunt and torture me for the rest of my life. I was now paying the price for having held the girl of my dreams in my arms with a broken heart.

I guess Jackie had dreams and aspirations too, and they obviously did not include me. I couldn't really blame her for striving for something better than I could offer her from a materialistic standpoint, but no man—and I mean no man—could ever have loved her to the extent that I loved Jackie Dee Stone. My love for Jackie had no borders or boundaries, and there was simply no standard of measurement in the universe with which to compare it.

Every time I saw Jackie coming and going from her house across Chelsea Street after our breakup, it was a constant reminder to me of a life with her that had slipped through my fingers through no fault of my own notwithstanding. I liked taking long walks in the rain in those days after I lost her because no one could see the teardrops running down my face. It was during one of these walks that I surmised that if there were some higher power behind my glance into the future and seeing Jackie and I together. And if it was really meant for us to be together—then I simply must sit back and wait for Jackie Dee to come back to me. If we really were each other's destinies, she would.

Jackie had asked me not to interfere with her new life, and so I did just as she had requested. As difficult as it was for me, I did not call, write, or approach Jackie for the next seven months. Now and then, I considered writing to her and sharing what I had been feeling for her all those years—my dreams, everything. First of all, just to let her know how deep my feelings for her were, and then to see if she would even care. However, I felt like that may look like an act of desperation, and even though I did sit down and hand-write everything out one day, I chose not to send the letter. I went so far as to place the letter in an envelope and stamp it, but I never did mail it. I thought, no—if she were going to come back to me, it had to be of her own volition and not because she felt obligated by something I had experienced almost seven years ago.

One time in the middle of January of 1977, I was warming the car up for my mother when Jackie came walking across the street, opened up the passenger door of the car, and got in. I thought, "Lord, if I am dreaming, please never let me wake up." This was the closest I had been to her in a couple of months.

Jackie asked me how I'd been doing since she'd ripped my heart out of my chest, thrown it on the ground, stomped on it, and then picked it up and tried to force-feed it to me.

Actually, in all sincerity, she just wanted to say hello and see how I was doing. We talked about everything except what I really wanted to talk about. I told Jackie that I missed seeing her and that she looked gorgeous beyond words, when just then her seductive body fragrance zapped me once again, making me lightheaded and dizzy. We did not get to talk for very long because she had to go.

The next four or five months were the most difficult of my life. When I was not on the job, I managed to stay drunk or high quite a bit of the time. I found it difficult to want to do anything, whether it was going to work or working out lifting weights, something I had always loved to do. In the mornings, I occasionally played Russian roulette with my revolver. In the evenings, I was usually so drunk or high that I would slip in and out of consciousness.

I tried to hold down two or three jobs to keep my mind occupied and keep myself busy, but it didn't work. I took my frustrations about losing her out on others who were looking for trouble anyway. During this time, I had my share of run-ins with the law, court costs, fines, lawyer's fees, and restitution fees. I got into a lot of fights, crashed a few cars, and did some damage here and there. Nothing could cure me of the Jackie blues; it didn't matter how much alcohol I drank, how many drugs I took, or how much damage I caused to other people and their possessions. There was simply no peace to be found anywhere except at the cemetery, as you will see later on.

Over the next couple of months, I overdosed on drugs. I consumed so much alcohol that sometimes I would have no recollection the next day of burning down someone's house or smashing up a car by flipping it end over end right onto someone's front porch. I remember standing before a judge in a courtroom, not knowing what I had been arrested for or even what I was being accused of.

Sometimes I'd be behind the wheel of a car and at the drop of a hat, regardless of who was in the car, I would suddenly hit the gas, work the car up to speed, and then yank the steering wheel one way or another, causing the car to roll repeatedly. I can remember doing this at least twice. On several occasions, while leaving one drinking establishment or another, I would vow to myself that I would run every red light on my way home. Sometimes I would make it home without incident, and other times I would broadside another vehicle or get hit myself. I was a teenager completely surrounded in constant turmoil, and anything but stable. I was now in full vigor of being a product of the environment around me, which was altogether destructive as well as pitiful.

I am not going to spend a lot of time writing about every little detail of my self-degradation through substance abuse. That is not what this story is about. But without Jackie Dee's presence in my life, just know that I was dying inside.

It got to the point where I simply could not stand to look at myself in the mirror or even hear the sound of my own voice. I had lost all of my self-worth without Jackie Dee in my life. I lost a lot of weight because sometimes I would not eat or sleep for days on end. I was a walking zombie. My mind was in a fog all the time, and I did not know if I was coming or going. At times, it became difficult for me to distinguish between my imagination and reality. I just could not pick myself up off the deck and shake it off. The thought and realization of losing Jackie Dee would just pull me back down into utter despair and depression again and again.

I just cannot explain the powerful, gripping effect that Jackie Dee had on my life. No matter what I tried to do, I could not stop the life from being drained right out of me. I could not understand where this force or energy was coming from that kept me spellbound and mesmerized over Jackie Dee. At no fault of my own did I do anything to bring this on. I did not ask for this—it just happened.

Living across the street from the girl of my dreams carried with it the added bonus of seeing the person for whom she had left me for—pick her up in the morning to take her to school.

I watched the two of them one morning as he helped her slide across the icy sidewalk from the front of her house to his car. Talk about being in torment, my God it just killed me to think of her being with anyone else but me, let alone to have to witness it to that I had to just turn away. Good heavens, enough of that little piece of memory!

One night, late in the evening, I was sitting on my front porch knocking down a couple of cold beers. As I looked across the street at Jackie's house, I began remembering that one evening that I'd hoped and prayed that I would be able to see her somehow. The night she had actually come outside and passed me that note. Only now, if she were to come outside, it would not be to see me. As I sat there, I remember how sad it made me feel just at the very thought of that.

My friend John, whom I'd known since the second grade, came pulling up to my house and joined me there on my porch. He kept trying to get me to smoke some new kind of grass that was blowing through town that month. I refused at first, and then finally said what the hell.

Later on around one-thirty in the morning the bar on the corner was beginning to close. We could see people coming outside. Some were practically crawling to their cars, thinking they were somehow going to drive home. Shortly thereafter, as John and I sat there drinking and smoking, we heard a woman scream. We looked up in the direction of the bar, and we saw two men assaulting this woman.

My friend John said, "That looks like Norman and Pete."

Norman and Pete were two well-known, middle-aged hell-raisers and troublemakers on the east side. In my book, there were just two low-life, wannabe bikers.

I said to John, "I think you're right, and I think that's Sam they're slapping around up there."

Sam was a girl who also lived on the east side. She was engaged to and living with a close friend of ours named Kenny.

I said, "Come on, John, let's go up there and help her."

John said, "Daniel, that's Norman and Pete up there; they'll kill you."

I said, "I'm going up there with or without you. What's it gonna be?"

John reluctantly came with me, and we took off running up to the corner. As we got closer to them, we saw that they were ripping Sam's blouse off, lifting her off the ground by her hair, and slapping her across the face. I started yelling at them to stop what they were doing in an effort to draw their attention away from Sam and toward us.

Pete continued abusing Sam, but Norman turned his attention toward us. I began yelling and cussing at Norman and Pete to pick on someone their own size instead of beating up on this girl.

Norman, pointing his finger at me yelled, "You are not a part of this; this doesn't concern you. Turn around and walk away, now!"

I yelled at Norman and called him a pussy, and then I said, "I bet I can take you right here and now, you worthless piece of shit!" Behind him, I could see Pete continuing to pull Sam by the hair and pouring beer all over her. Then he slugged her, knocking her unconscious and to the ground.

I began to move in closer to Norman to try to get the drop on him and connect with at least the first punch. I spit in Norman's face as I swung my fist at him, but it only connected with a glancing blow because John got in between us. As John began yelling at me that we needed to get the hell out of there, Norman punched me in the side of the head. Then he punched John in the face, knocking him over the hood of a car.

As I staggered backwards holding my head, I yelled, "Oh, you motherfucker!" Then I drew the gun I was carrying, pointed it at Norman, and fired off a round in his direction, just missing him.

Norman hollered, "You just signed your death warrant, son!"

I yelled, "I'm not your damn son!" Then I fired a round into the saddlebag on his motorcycle.

I walked up to Norman, stuck the gun in his face, and said, "I will shoot you where you stand, you piece of shit, if you both don't get the hell out of here right now—what's it gonna be?"

His brother Pete grabbed Norman by the back of his collar and said, "Some other time, man—let's go!" They both got on their motorcycles, started them up, and took off rumbling down the street.

As I started to make my way over to see if Sam was okay, John got in my face and punched me in the chest. He said, "They are going to get us good man, just you wait and see."

I pointed the gun at John's face and said, "Don't you ever do that shit again!"

John said, "Oh, are you going to shoot me—your friend?"

I pulled the hammer back, cocking it. Then I yelled at John, "Run away, run away now!"

John took off running down the street to his car, dodging side to side just in case I decided to fire off a shot in his direction.

I swear it seemed like any time I smoked grass, it made me irritable, angry and brought out my more aggressive side. But I was upset with John for two reasons. First of all, he had been no help to me in this particular situation, which was rare for John; he had always been reliable in the past. The other reason was that he had punched me hard in the chest.

Sam was still out cold, and I tried to help her up, grabbing her purse and things. I could see no serious injuries on her, just bumps and bruises. Then I carried her down the street to my car. I placed Sam in the front seat of my car, and then proceeded to drive her home. As I drove up in front of her house, Sam's boyfriend, Kenny, came outside and approached the vehicle. I got out of the car and began walking around to the passenger side to help Sam out. But when Kenny saw Sam slumped over in the front seat, he began yelling at me and pushing me around. I thought, "Oh shit, here we go again." Fortunately, I was able to get Kenny to calm down long enough to explain to him what had happened. In the end, Kenny thanked me for saving Sam; God only knows what those two were planning to do to her that night. Kenny also reminded me that Norman and Pete weren't likely to forget about me any time soon.

In an unrelated incident, Sam was the victim of a gunshot wound to the head a couple of years later. I'm not sure if the shooter was ever identified and apprehended for murdering her or not. These kinds of violent crimes happened all the time around our neighborhood. It was difficult to keep from taking matters into your own hands and taking some kind of action against what was happening all around us.

During this period of my life, I spent a lot of time in the cemetery at night. It became my home away from home, and was the place where I drank alcohol and took drugs of all kinds. I liked hanging out in the shadows of the tombs at night. If there was any peace to be found for me, it was at the cemetery. I know there was nothing there in the dark recesses of the cemetery at night that was not there when the sunlight was shining during the day. To put it another way, there is nothing in a darkened room that is not there when the light is turned on. But it was still a comfort to me to visit the cemetery, and I did find some peace and relaxation there just the same.

I usually went to the cemetery where my father was buried, but I sometimes went to other cemeteries in the area as well. I would stay there in my car all night, taking drugs and drinking alcohol and thinking about Jackie Dee. During this dark period of my life, I began to develop strong dependencies on all this stuff I was putting into my body. Over time, my tolerance level for drugs and alcohol had increased tremendously. This meant that I had to take a little more drugs and drink a little more alcohol each time to get that numbing effect that I so desperately needed.

On at least two occasions, Jackie called me up to ask if she could borrow some of my albums for some party that she and Mark were going to. At the time, I had a pretty good collection of records; it got me invited to parties quite a bit just so I could play disc jockey while everyone else partied to the music I played for them.

Obviously, I let Jackie Dee borrow whatever she wanted for as long as she needed it. You see, I was still so spellbound and hypnotized by my love for Jackie Dee that I would have been willing to do anything she asked.

Even during this dark period of my life, the vision I had seen years earlier of Jackie and me together was still bright, vivid, and immutable in my heart and mind. I just could not let go of it. I would not keel over no matter how many drugs I took. I would not die no matter how many car wrecks I was in or how much damage I sustained to my body by fighting and brawling about.

One day after Jackie had borrowed some of my albums, she came over and knocked on my door and asked me for a ride to work. I told her I would be glad to drive her there. At the time, I had a '64 Ford Fairlaine; she jumped into my car, and off we went. Jackie worked at Hav-a-Snack Restaurant, which was located on the corner of 27th and Hardesty. As I drove her to work that day, the two of us had a pretty good talk, and we continued our conversation once we arrived. Call it wishful thinking on my part, but I thought I could sense a connection between us during our conversation that seemed to ignite a spark in Jackie. There was a gleam that appeared in her eye and in that smile of hers every time she made reference to the two of us that gave me a glimmer of hope.

Not long after that, I was driving up Hardesty Street when Jackie spotted me and waved me over. She had just gotten off work and asked if I would give her ride home. I told her that I would be more than happy to give her a lift. She wanted me to stop along the way so she could get a pack of smokes at 7-Eleven, so we stopped, I bought her a pack of Marlborough 100 cigarettes and a Coke, and then we drove on home.

It was probably about a month or so after that day that I heard the news that Jackie and Mark were engaged. When I heard that gut-wrenching, heartbreaking, tragic piece of news, made worse by the fact that I had been drinking rather heavily that morning, I began to play my favorite game, Russian Roulette. However, first I tore up the note that I had written to Jackie but never mailed that explained everything from her smile to my vision and …

Just then, I heard a knock at my front door. I put the gun down on the kitchen table and answered the door. It was my friend John, whom I had not seen since the night I had stuck the gun in his face. I invited him in, and then the phone rang, so I went to answer it. The call was for my brother, who was not home at the time. All of a sudden, I heard the gun discharge in the kitchen. I dropped the phone, ran into the kitchen, grabbed the gun from John's hand, and asked him if he was okay.

He said, "I'm okay, but damn, I didn't know that gun was loaded! I saw it lying there on the table and picked it up." He had pointed it at the floor and squeezed the trigger, and it went off, shooting a hole in the floor.

I said, "You dope. I think that bullet was meant for me."

John invited me over to his place for some drinks with him and his girlfriend, Sharon. I accepted his invitation, and I let John drive my car to his place since I had just been cited for my second D.U.I. in as many weeks. I had also already put away quite a bit of alcohol that morning.

It turned out that John's girlfriend had a sister name Linda. I did not know she was going to be there as well, or I probably would have bowed out. John was determined to do everything in his power to keep me from being left alone, for obvious reasons.

Linda kept playing the same song, *Blinded by the Light* by Manfred Mann, over and over again. When I couldn't take it anymore, I stepped out onto the front patio. I began thinking about how long I could go on living like this and wondered whether my days were numbered. My thoughts quickly shifted to wondering what Jackie was doing at that very moment. Standing there on the patio and staring off into the night, I remember feeling as if I had been all hollowed out inside. I was thinking of going to the cemetery that night, where I could be by myself, lost in my thoughts with my drugs and alcohol.

Just then, Linda came out onto the patio and started to come close to me. I turned away from her, but she came even closer and kissed me on the cheek. Yes, I may have been vulnerable or off guard or whatever, but I shoved Linda back, and I went back inside.

She followed behind me in close pursuit. I headed straight for the record player that was playing that same song over and over. I snatched the record up off the turntable, turned around, and broke the album over Linda's head, then shoved her back into a chair.

As she hit the chair and then the floor, she yelled, "Ouch, I think you just broke my ankle!" Sharon had to take Linda to the hospital for treatment, but her ankle was only sprained. By the time they all got back from the hospital, I was so drunk that I could not drive myself back home. They loaded me into my car and drove me home.

I was not then or at any other time interested in any other girl besides Jackie Dee. No other girl could turn my head, let alone capture my attention. As far as I would ever be concerned, there was not a girl on the entire planet who could hold a candle to my little girl, Jackie Dee.

6

The Dream Suffers Another Crushing, Near-Fatal Blow

Up until this point in time, it seemed like an eternity since our break up, when it was really only about seven months. And in June of 1977, guess who came knocking at my front door? It was none other than Little Miss Jackie Dee. I opened the door and said, "Jackie, what a pleasant surprise; you have no idea how good it is to see you again." Jackie asked if she could come inside because she needed to talk to me about something very important.

I could feel my heart starting to swell up inside of me with the excitement of seeing her face to face again. I wanted to wrap my arms around her and kiss her just like I had the first time I'd kissed those lips behind that seductive smile of hers. But without seeming too overzealous, I said, "Yes, come on in and have a seat."

When she walked into the room, I thought, "My God, she's even more beautiful then she was when I last saw her." Yet, I could sense that something was different about her; but what was it?

Jackie sat down on a footstool close to where I had just positioned myself, and it rather surprised me that she sat so close to me. Nevertheless, it felt terrific to be so close to her again, that I just wanted to reach out and touch her hair as it lay upon her shoulders. Just then, I could detect her lovely body fragrance and then it began to make me dizzy. I thought, "Oh no, here we go again." I shook it off and composed myself the best I could so that I could give her my full attention and hear what she had to say.

Jackie asked me what I had been up to and wanted to know if I was seeing anyone. When she asked me that, I got the sense that she was feeling me out to see where my interests lie concerning her. As we sat there having our discussion and Jackie asked me things concerning where things stood between us, it's hard for me to put into words the hope that filled my heart. The conversation had me thinking that I might have a chance to hold this vision of beauty in my arms once again. At the same time, I wondered whether this was some sort of a tease or a game she was playing with my heart.

I fought long and hard to keep the dam that had formed around my heart once again from breaking open, but at the same time, I could not take my eyes off of Jackie Dee. I played it cool and told Jackie that I missed seeing her and that I had just been working, keeping myself busy. What I did not tell Jackie was that I had been going out of my ever-loving mind over her.

I asked her how things had been going between her and Mark. Jackie said she did not want to talk about it, so I said, "Okay." She asked if it was okay for her to smoke a cigarette, and I said, "Well, of course it is." She pulled out a cigarette, and I lit it for her. And suddenly, Jackie came right out and asked me straight up if I still liked her.

I thought, "The girl of my dreams is asking me if I still like her." Imagine that—*like* her. I didn't want to reveal my hand just yet about how crazy I really was about this vision of beauty sitting there before me, nor did I want to seem overzealous about the whole matter. So I told Jackie that I still cared for her and that if it were possible, I would very much like to start seeing her again.

Boy, talk about a watered-down reply! What I really wanted to say to Jackie was, "Jackie, I love you ever so much; please come back into my life, I'm lost without you." But I could not tell Jackie that I knew that deep down inside of my heart of hearts, my true feelings for her would be forever intact and immutable. I could not lay all my cards on the table before her for fear that if she really knew that I had been her prisoner of love since that first smile, she would somehow use it against me. I believed that if Jackie knew how hopelessly in love with her I really was, she might pursue whatever other avenues of romance she chose because she knew she would always have me there to fall back on.

I just didn't know what to think any more about matters in which my heart was concerned. I was extremely vulnerable around Jackie Dee, and truth be told, I always had been.

As we sat there conversing in my living room that day, I felt I had to make a concentrated effort to wall up my true feelings of just how hopelessly in love I was with Jackie Dee. I can remember my mind running away with itself and thinking that if I were to reveal my true feelings for her, she might take advantage of me in so many ways. That would no doubt have driven me to the point of no return or recovery. So, I decided to keep everything—and I mean every thought, dream, and vision, even the incident about her smile that blew me away so long ago—all to myself. I shared it with no one for the next thirty years.

I considered that if I hadn't revealed these secrets concerning how I felt about Jackie Dee the first time we were together, and our breakup had literally taken me to the brink of death's door. So I could only imagine what might happen this time around if I were to open up my heart to her and share my innermost secrets. I have always had this gift, which is really a curse—that enables me to internalize everything. So, for the next thirty-some years, I garrisoned my heart and mind, keeping all my heartfelt secrets about her hidden and buried deep inside me. At the time, I thought that only on my deathbed would I share what had occurred as I stood there across the street from Jackie Dee so long ago, when I was captured and consumed by her smile. Besides, who would have believed it anyway, or even cared?

However, the conversation that Jackie and I were having right there in my living room was moving along in a most positive fashion. It seemed that things were definitely shaping up for us to get back together again. Jackie asked me if I would meet her later that night at the Minute Circle Community Center, which was just a few blocks away from where we lived, to discuss all of this further. She said she wanted to meet up with me there, before we continued on to her friend Penny's house that lived nearby, where we could really spend some time together and talk.

Suddenly, Jackie jumped up and said she had to go. And as she was getting ready to make her exit, she turned, threw her arms around me, and held me close to her. Then she gazed into my eyes and pressed her lips against mine.

For a brief moment, I was carried away and thought I had died and gone to heaven. She definitely caught me off guard with that kiss. I never saw it coming, but she most certainly got my heart rate elevated and my hormones all in an uproar. As we stood there holding and kissing each other ever so affectionately, the thought came to me that just months before, I'd been right there in almost the same spot, dying on the telephone. Now I was being resuscitated with her kiss—it was like she breathed life back into me.

Jackie's kiss did just that, actually. It brought me back to life again and gave me the hope I needed to go on. I simply could not believe it was really happening, but it was. I thought, "Hallelujah!" as I held Jackie Dee in my arms, never wanting to let her go. I wanted to make the kiss last for as long as I possibly could. I finally let her up for some air and walked her out onto my front porch, where we used to sit and talk as far back as the summer of 1974. We just kept staring at each other as she turned to go, and so I asked her, "Do you really have to go?"

Jackie said, "Yes, but I'll see you later."

With utter amazement, I watched her walk across the street with that little side-to-side hitch she had in her walk. When she reached her front porch, she turned to wave and blow me a kiss before she went into the house. I caught it and put it in my wallet, and it is still there to this day.

I fell back inside my house and dropped down onto the sofa, pondering over all that had just taken place. However, I still could not help thinking that something seemed different about her, but what was it? Jackie had seemed fairly uninhibited about expressing herself, but from the first time I saw her face when I answered the door, I could sense that something was different or perhaps something was missing.

Before I proceed with our story, I want the reader to know that it gives me no earthly pleasure to write about something as sensitive, personal, and private as what I'm about to share. However, there is absolutely no way of leaving out this next portion of the story and yet still remain true and forthright to the story, so readers, beware.

All of a sudden, it came to me; I was about 99 percent sure I knew what was missing, and it stabbed me straight through the heart. Yes, it was that one most precious treasure that a girl can only give away once in her entire lifetime—her virginity.

Now, I suspected that there was a possibility this might happen while Jackie and I were apart. Nevertheless, every night as I held her close in my dreams, I would pray, "Please God, please God no, don't let this happen; please keep the girl of my dreams a chaste virgin for me, as I have vowed to keep myself pure for her." Sadly, my suspicions would be confirmed before the night was over.

As the reality of this god-awful tragedy began to settle into my heart and mind, I began to cry in anger, sobbing uncontrollably like the fool that I was. I don't know how, but somehow I just knew. Not only was I having a hard time coping with the loss of my father even to this point in time, but I was also still on the mend from having my heart broken by losing Jackie Dee just months earlier. And now, it appeared that Jackie was coming back to me, but minus that one very special gift that life has to offer just once and that I had believed would most certainly be mine one day. Son of a bitch!

I tried to lift myself up off the sofa and tried for the life of me to shake it off, but I simply could not. I can't explain it, nor do I think anyone out there could relate to why this affected me in such a devastating, heart-wrenching way. It left me shell-shocked down to the very core of my being, and I even contemplated taking my own life right then and there.

To make matters worse, I suddenly began to feel a tremendous pain inside my chest, as my heart rate began to accelerate. It felt like someone had placed a tremendous weight on my chest and was crushing the life right out of me, similar to how I'd felt when Jackie had broken up with me. Once again, there wasn't a damn thing I could do to stop what was happening to me. The pain that was crushing me was worse than any kind of pain I had ever experienced before. Where was it coming from, and why was this happening to me?

As my heartbeat began to get completely out of control, I tried to think about something else in an attempt to slow it down, but I could not. I thought, "My god, what dark path is my heart taking me down now?" I was uncontrollably hyperventilating and could not catch my breath, and I suddenly became so physically ill that I began to vomit all over the place.

I thought, "I'm not going to survive this, am I, Lord? God forgive me, I must be in hell ..."

I must have blacked out; I lost time, and there were a couple of hours that I could not account for. To make matters worse, as embarrassing as it is for me to admit, I had wet all over myself. This sort of attack or seizure had happened at least two other times that I could remember, but why?

When I woke up, I felt like I had been run over and shit on by a herd of elephants. I may have even suffered a slight stroke that day. I survived whatever kind of attack it was, but all I could think about was the reality of the situation; from that day forth, from a sexual standpoint, I would always be number two in the life of the girl of my dreams. Moreover, there wasn't a damn thing I or anyone else could do about it. Not even God

Himself could restore her virginity; it was gone forever. This thought riddled my body with bullets of pain, despair, and loss; it was my loss, and I could never get it back. To this day—some thirty years later—I still have not recovered from this tremendous loss. It has plagued me throughout the years, it has tortured my thoughts, and it has haunted me in my dreams.

Just a reminder to the readers who have stuck with me this far: this is one of the reasons why I am bearing my soul within these pages.

In doing so, it is my hope that it will at least partially cure what ails me and relieve some of the pain that still wounds and cripples my heart, mind, and even my very soul after all these years.

I had always known that there were three things that God could not do. One, God could not lie. Two, he could not make anyone serve him. Three, he could not remember your past sins once they were under the blood of Christ. But there was a fourth. God could not restore Jackie Dee's virginity.

If I had not seen the vision of us together, the day I was captured by Jackie Dee's smile, and had I not experienced the gamut of emotions and the euphoria that followed. Not to mention all the precious moments we did share together. I am positive that this would not have had such a devastating effect on me. But as it was, it felt like a part of me had died, and there wasn't a damn thing I could do about it. To make matters worse, the notes that Jackie had hand-written for me just the previous summer stating that I would be the first one to make love to her kept resurfacing in my mind. To the point that I started to get that sick feeling coming over me again so much that I just wanted to crawl away somewhere and die. So, what was left of my dream now that the most important facet of it could never be fulfilled?

I began to question what I had experienced so long ago, when we were kids. If it was destiny for us to be together—if there was a predetermined course of events that would unite us—then why wasn't it ever revealed to her like it was to me? I don't think Jackie Dee was ever even grazed by Cupid's arrow as far as I was concerned. Where I on the other hand, had been pierced threw by what felt like an army of bow toting Cupid's from all directions, much like General Custer was at Little Bighorn. Neither he nor I ever had a chance, but there was one difference: he died, and I was taken prisoner—Jackie Dee's prisoner of love—forever.

I guess the bottom line is that my heart became hardened in so many ways that I began to question every thought and emotion I had concerning Jackie, and soon I became cold and callused. I didn't like what was happening to me, but there wasn't anything I could do to keep from feeling that way. I truly felt like a part of my heart had shut down and died that day. Neither drugs nor alcohol nor God nor even the passage of time could ever heal the pain and suffering that was consuming me over this tragic loss.

I am sad to say that for the next quarter of a century, I was pretty much unable to express any human emotions concerning these matters. I kept them all internalized until right now as I write these pages. I could write volumes about the pain and nightmares concerning this issue that has affected me to this very day, but I will stop for now and get on with the story.

After cleaning up my mess from the seizure, I started in again by drinking a couple of beers before Jackie and I met up. Just as we had planned, I watched and waited for her to leave her house so I could head out my back door and meet her. I cut over to the next block behind my house, which was Poplar Street, rounded the corner, and caught up with Jackie on 24th and Lister. We thought it was best to leave secretly and separately; we didn't want her parents to see us together for the same reasons they had played a part in splitting Jackie and I up the first damn time.

As we were walking down 24th Street together, I noticed that Jackie kept looking back over her shoulder. Finally, I asked her why she kept looking behind her. Jackie said she was afraid that her ex-boyfriend Mark would come driving up and see us together.

I said, "That shit-hole! So, the two of you are broken up now? I thought you were engaged." Before Jackie could answer, I went on to ask her, "Do you want to tell me about it now?"

Jackie said that she had broken off the engagement with Mark because things just weren't working out and that she wanted to start seeing me again.

I said, "Okay, then don't you worry your pretty little head about him."

I went on to tell Jackie, "If he does drive by and happens to see the two of us together, trust me, there is no way in hell he will ever slow down, let alone stop.

It would be his second-to-last stop before entering his final resting place—the grave." I told Jackie to believe me, that she was safe with me.

I was actually hoping like hell that Mark would drive by and stop; I was so full of anger and rage that night that I wanted to cave his damn face in and twist his head off right in front of her. And believe it or not, the son of a bitch did drive by that night and saw the two of us together, but he did not slow down, let alone stop. He just kept on going. As he drove by us, for his pleasure and viewing purposes, I displayed—well let's just say an unpleasant hand gesture.

Jackie and I also saw her ex-boyfriend drive by us a couple of other times as we walked along 24th Street on other nights, but he always kept on going. The last time we saw him drive by us, he actually waved to us. Nevertheless, each time we saw Mark drive by, I couldn't keep from displaying my middle finger to him.

Anyway, as we were walking to her friend Penny's house that night, Jackie went on to say that Mark was very domineering. He was always trying to change her into something that she wasn't, and she also suspected that he might be seeing someone else. Jackie also said that her parents were really bearing down hard on her and that she felt like they would not let her have a life of her own. They were constantly quarreling with her over one thing or another, and they would not let her have any freedom to do the things she wanted to do.

Just then, Jackie grabbed me and began kissing me, and as she was kissing me, she began to tremble. I held her firmly in my arms to calm her, and I told her that everything was going to be okay now that she was back in my arms again. Just a simple little kiss from Jackie Dee's lips and having her back in my arms really got things emotionally ignited between us. Not only were we all over each other just like we had always wanted to do when we were first emotionally involved with each other, but now there didn't seem to be any inhibitions to stop us from expressing how we felt.

I leaned Jackie up against the wall of the community center. As I looked into her eyes and began to kiss her on the lips and face over and over again, she whispered something to me. She said, "I'm spending the night with my friend Penny tonight, and I want you to spend the night there with me."

I thought to myself, "Oh ... my ... God," but then said to her, "You bet your ass I will."

Jackie and I were all over each other all the way to Penny's house. We must have stopped ten times to work in a kiss here and there before we finally arrived. Penny lived just four blocks away from where we lived. Penny and her mother, Mary, were nice people, and they welcomed me into their home. They raved on about how nice-looking and handsome I was—pleeee-ase. Penny said to Jackie, "And this is the guy you left for that creep-face? Girl, you're craaaazy; he's gorgeous!"

The four of us visited for a while in the living room, as Jackie and I waited to be alone with great anticipation. Finally, Penny said to Jackie and me, "Let's go upstairs."

She led Jackie and me upstairs and into her bedroom. Then she said, "I'll check in on the two of you later; I'm sure you have lots to talk about." Then she left the room, closing the bedroom door behind her, and leaving Jackie and me alone at last. I was surprised that Penny's mom wasn't lurking about and that she allowed us such privacy. However, Mary was a very open-minded person and she pretty much let us do whatever we wanted.

Immediately, without speaking a word, Jackie and I came together like two freight trains colliding head-on. Once again, we were all over each other, kissing and embracing. Hour after hour passed, as we spent this time getting reacquainted and making up for lost time.

Jackie Dee was all over me so much that I could hardly catch my breath. She was putting her hands all over me. After a while,

I could tell by the way Jackie was coming on to me that she was definitely ready to do more than just make out with me.

It was during that night and the following morning that we also got everything we needed to say out into the open.

Sometime in the middle of that night, as Jackie and I were rehashing what had taken place while we were apart, Jackie told me she had had sex with her ex-boyfriend Mark. She could only remember doing it once. She said she had been drinking that night and could remember very little about it, but that it did happen.

I wanted so very much to believe her, but whether it happened just once or more than once did nothing to ease my pain or my feelings of the loss over what I felt should have been mine. Now, I had already come to this conclusion earlier that day, and somehow I just knew in my heart that Jackie wasn't a virgin anymore, but hearing it from her lips pierced right through me. I tried to fight back the tears that were forming in my eyes, but to no avail; sadness began to envelop me.

As we sat there talking that night, I told Jackie that I could sense that something was different about her when I'd first seen her in my living room earlier that day, but at the time I didn't tell her what it was. In reality, Jackie now seemed less refined in her mannerisms and rougher in her character. I knew that I had a potty-mouth, but Jackie cussed a lot more now, and that look of innocence she once had in her eyes just wasn't there anymore. I could tell right off that the months she had spent with Mark had not made her a better person, and I hated him for it. I hated him for what he had taken from her and from me. Jackie just wasn't the same girl she was just months before.

But regardless of what was missing inside of her or how she had changed, my love for her had not diminished in the least. I was still so very attracted and drawn to Jackie, and I was still so very much in love with her. I mean, even if she had slept with the entire varsity football team, she still would always have been the girl of my dreams. The fact remained that my love for Jackie was immeasurable and immutable, just as before. I told Jackie that I had not been with anyone else or even come close to having a relationship in any way, form, or fashion.

When I pressed Jackie that night about why she had slept with that shit-ass, she said, "But Daniel, we were engaged." I thought, "Oh boy, did I walk right into that one." Her honest and truthful reply just pricked my heart even more. If I could just keep my mouth shut, maybe I wouldn't get hurt so much.

Well, they say time heals all wounds—bullshit! Maybe it heals some physical wounds, but not the breaking or scarring of the heart, at least not my heart on matters where Jackie Dee was concerned. The bottom line was that this experience caused me to harden my heart from expressing any of my emotions to Jackie; regarding the things I had seen concerning the two of us so many years ago, for the next thirty years.

When Jackie mentioned being engaged, she could tell that I was crushed, as she could see the tears forming in my eyes and the strained look on my face. She began to do what she could to change the subject and talk about something else in an effort to try to get my mind off it. Penny checked in on us from time to time, and it seemed like every time she peeked in, either Jackie or I was crying. Penny would always say, "I'm sorry, I just wanted to check and see if either of you was thirsty or needed anything."

From that night on, Jackie and I were officially back together again. We were together every possible waking hour. We both shed a lot of tears that night as we got many things out in the open. However, from that point on, I became very cautious and guarded about my feelings for Jackie. Because of what she had put me through and the depths of despair I had sunk down to from when I had lost her before. Lastly, this experience had changed me now to where I became suspicious in my nature, and concerning what her true feelings were for me. I just felt that she could pull the plug on our relationship any time she wanted, so I proceeded with caution.

On July 20 of 1977, Jackie Dee turned fourteen years old. For her birthday, I gave her a clock radio and a camera, which I really bought so that I could take pictures of her.

That night, Jackie and I went to the drive-in with the very same friend of mine whom I had punched in the jaw the night that Jackie and I had first kissed. Mike was home on leave from the military with his wife, whom he had met and married over in Germany, where they were both stationed. Jackie and I did not see even five minutes of whatever was playing that night; we were all over each other as if we hadn't seen each other in six months. You would have thought it was I who had returned home on leave, considering the way Jackie and I were conducting ourselves. I knew it was rude for us to be all over each other right there in front of or I should say in the back seat of Mike's car. However, her folks were really tightening their grip on what Jackie could and could not do, so we took advantage of every available opportunity to express how we felt about each other. While we were in my friend's back seat that night, the flames of passion within us were burning so strongly that we came pretty close to doing something more than just making out.

Shortly after that night, the time came when Jackie Dee really wanted to make love with me. I still had strong reservations about doing this because Jackie was only fourteen years old. On the other hand I can remember thinking, as bad as this is going to sound, a part of me just didn't care anymore since she had already broken her vow to me. I was torn between trying to hold on to what was left of my crumpled-up dream and accepting the fact that I would never be her first and only lover.

One night, Jackie was spending the night with Penny, with whom she spent the night a lot of the time. At Penny's house, Jackie could pretty much be herself, smoking cigarettes and doing just about whatever she wanted. And now that I was back in the picture, we could spend some quality time together there at Penny's house. Jackie had purchased this two-piece, lavender, silk nightgown just for that night.

For the life of me, I desperately wanted Jackie Dee that night; she looked so enticingly beautiful. She was coming on to me as if she had been down this path before, and she knew exactly what to do. This not only bothered me, but it also distracted me; I was still a virgin at nineteen years old, if you can believe it. In those days and in that neighborhood, that simply was unheard of.

As redundant as this is going to sound, on that particular night, all I could think about was the fact that Jackie had offered herself up to someone else before me. She had given away that one most precious gift that I thought one day would be mine. The fact that she was still only fourteen years old was not helping matters either. These thoughts that kept bombarding my mind would not allow me to follow through with her that evening. Jackie was doing everything possible to arouse me, but I could not do a thing.

I have never been able to tell Jackie Dee the real reason why I could not follow through with her on that night. I acted like I was drunk when in reality I just could not get it out of my head that she wasn't a virgin anymore and that sexually, I would always be the number two person in her life. I could never look at Jackie in the same light as I had before because of what was now missing. Call it a loss of innocence, but I call it my loss, really. She'd given herself up at my expense, and I was paying for it with a broken heart. God help me, but I felt that no matter how much time passed, every time I looked at her, it would be a constant reminder of what could never be mine. Jackie was away from me long enough to give up that one thing that I felt would have bound us together forever.

For me then, and throughout the rest of my life, this was by far the worst thing that ever happened to me. After all, this was the girl of my dreams. Had I not experience all that I did in those early days concerning her, I am positive that none of this would be killing me inside like it was and indeed did. It would plague, hinder, and hamper our relationship for years to come, and it took on a life of its own. It would not allow me to be myself, and I felt like I could not relax in our relationship. Instead, I felt like I had to be on guard most of the time.

It also kept me from being able to share with Jackie Dee my deepest most heartfelt emotions concerning all I had experience in those early days as if they never even happened.

I stepped up my substance abuse to try to suppress my heartache and anger concerning the matter. However, when I was under the influence of drugs or alcohol, the pain that I kept trying to internalize would sometimes surface and cause me to lash out at whoever happened to be standing close by. I sometimes became despondent and depressed. I just could not seem to shake it off, and I could never tell Jackie why. Besides, there was nothing she or anyone could do to restore what had been taken from me.

For whatever reason, the pain I felt in my heart over this loss was equal to the pain of losing a loved one. It just disgust me so much, and it still does to this day. I am still haunted in my dreams over her broken promises, about how she left me a month after the passing of my father when I really could have used her support, and on and on. These things have never left me.

If there is one thing that life has taught me, it is that I have no control over these heart-wrenching memories. They have taken on a life of their own, and there is nothing I can do to stop them this side of the grave, which is probably when the heartaches and nightmares will finally end. God knows I can only hope so. If I could be so fortunate as to be granted one wish, I would not wish for eternal life, fame, or fortune; I would wish to have the girl of my dreams—Jackie Dee, back as a chaste virgin. I swear to God that if there should ever come a day when I take my own life, it will be for this reason. I simply cannot get over the fact that I was not Jackie Dee's first and only lover.

It is my hope, that in writing about my most inner, heartfelt emotions that it will help me somehow, in some way, no matter how small it may be.

Anyway, after our first, failed attempt to come together, I could not wait to see how Jackie would react to me the next day. I thought she might be distant towards me since I did not give her what she wanted. I thought that perhaps she would leave me again and go elsewhere. I just didn't know what to expect from her anymore.

Later that day, Jackie and I got together at Penny's house again. To my utter shock and amazement, Jackie was very loving and affectionate towards me, just as much as she had been the day before. This was really a relief for me, and it gave me hope to continue on.

That day, Jackie and I were playing around in Penny's bedroom, tickling each other and just being silly, when Jackie accidentally called me Mark. She quickly apologized and tried to make up for her mistake, but it had still gashed me pretty deeply. To even hear Jackie speak his name was most unbearable, and it was far worse yet to be called by that shit-head's name. I thought to myself, "You know, it's probably been less than a month since Jackie was last with him."

7

Paradise Restored!

All that week, Jackie and I had to sneak around so that we could see each other. If Jackie's parents found out that we were seeing each other again, they would use whatever means were necessary to split us up like they had the first time we were emotionally involved. Obviously, for the same reasons they tried and succeeded just the year before.

That next Friday, Jackie told her mom she was spending the night with Penny when in fact she was spending the night with me. My mom was out of town that weekend, and so we pretty much had the run of the house. Jackie left her house and walked to the corner as if she were walking to Penny's house. Then she went left on 24th Street rather than taking a right, the direction in which Penny lived. From there, Jackie headed over onto the next block, which was Poplar Street, cut through the yard behind my backyard, and came through the back door of my house. We had to keep the curtains drawn shut so that our nosy neighbors and her folks, who lived just across the street, wouldn't be able to spot her through the windows of my house.

Jackie and I started out that evening by taking pictures in my front living room while listening to music. We began cuddling each other ever so affectionately, when that soon gave way to such a display of emotional fireworks that it didn't take long before Jackie was leading me by the hand to my bedroom and into my bed. Jackie and I were all over each other, our clothes coming off left and right. I could see very quickly where this was going, and I thought, "Oh ... my ... God, here I go again."

I honestly felt that if I did not give Jackie what she wanted right then and there, I would be placing our relationship in jeopardy so much that she would probably leave me. How could I possibly explain it to Jackie this time around if I were not able to follow through with her on this night? Regardless of what was right or wrong and the havoc that my emotions were wreaking inside of me, and even though Jackie Dee was only fourteen years old, I simply could not resist her advances. She was just that irresistible to me. After all, Jackie Dee was my life's pursuit; she was in fact—the girl of my dreams. After nineteen years of saving myself for Jackie Dee for this very special moment, as I lay there beside her on my bed, I decided that it was finally time to let the dam around my heart—break wide open.

Jackie's beautiful soft skin pressing against mine and her warm body's seductive fragrance that was all around us had me hypnotized and spellbound. In my heart, I knew this was the moment I had waited for all my life. This was it.

As I positioned myself on top of her, my body began to make me a thousand promises that it would not let me down. Jackie and I began making love with such emotional fervor that you would thought this was to be our last time to ever make-love to one another, even though this would be our first. My God—I was completely immersed in Jackie's love as I could feel it enveloping me over and over again. All the while, I was letting it all go inside of her and loving her with every ounce of emotion that

I had been carrying around inside of me for her all these years. In my mind's eye, I was taken back to that very first day when I could see Jackie standing there and I saw her smile. I remember thinking how incredible that was. Just then, tears began to fill my eyes, but these were tears of joy and happiness. Basking in her love—I thought this was probably as close to heaven as I was ever going to be.

I know this was my first time, but I did not expect to feel this rush of sensually erotic emotions surging through my heart, mind, and body as we lay there making love. To tell the truth, I honestly didn't know what it was going to be or feel like, I just didn't know.

To say the least, it was incredibly pleasurable beyond what mere words can depict or define.

I had dreamed of coming together with Jackie so many times before that night, and now it was all coming true. If Jackie was experiencing a fraction of what was happening to me, it would definitely make this dream complete.

For hours on end, Jackie and I jockeyed around for that one position that would take us to another area of paradise that we had yet to explore. On this wondrous night, we were like two turbulent mountain streams coming together to form one smoothly flowing river. There is simply no superlative in the English lexicon that can describe the heights of love to which Jackie took me, but I think you know me well enough by now to know that I will try.

Being immersed ever so deeply in her love felt nothing short of perfect. It was just like it was meant to be, and even greater and more enthralling than I dreamt it would be. The very act of making love to Jackie Dee was like sheer poetry in motion. The love being exchanged between the two of us and the heights of human emotion that we attained and went beyond were more signs of affirmation to me that we were really meant to be together.

I wanted to go on feeling the way she was making me feel forever. Just like the first time we kissed, I saw fireworks, and I saw the sky parting like a scroll, but this time the cows drove off and yes, I felt the earth move too.

Somewhere in the wee hours of the night, as I held this vision of beauty in my arms while she loved me with all her might. She aroused me so much that I became so worked up that all of a sudden, I could feel virtue surging uncontrollably out of me and into her, and just then she let go as well, over and over again. From that night on, we had such an insatiable appetite for making love to each other that the flames of intense passion burning within us could never be satisfied or quenched.

Jackie and I made love for most of the night. We both were physically exhausted beyond words as well as emotionally drained. We lay there regaining our strength so that we could continue to go at it again and again, and then we fell asleep in each other's arms.

I had done some tough things in my life, like working heavy construction, wrestling, and running in a marathon, but nothing had ever wiped me out like Jackie Dee did that night. Our first time making love was truly extraordinary. Such would be the case any time we would ever come together.

As I was drifting off to sleep holding Jackie in my arms, all I kept thinking about was that I wanted so very much to somehow marry this girl, this girl of my dreams. But how could I when she was only fourteen years old? I don't know if there was a state in the union that would have allowed such a thing. In this country a hundred years ago, it was lawful for girls to marry at twelve, and it still is in many other countries around the world. However, this wasn't 1877 but 1977, and in this country, I would have been thrown in jail!

We both knew that Jackie's mother had married very young and had had a baby shortly thereafter. We also knew that just a year or so before, a close relative of mine had been married at fifteen, but she had been pregnant. In those days, you pretty much had to marry whenever a baby was involved, but Jackie was not even fifteen, and there was no baby in the picture.

In those days and in that neighborhood, guys and girls became sexually active at very early ages; it just seemed like relationships between people tended to start when they were young. I don't know if it was because we had lived through the psychedelic sixties drug culture or the seventies sex culture, with sex, drugs and rock-n-roll influencing the masses, but I bet that had something to do with it.

In any case, I tossed and turned over the perplexities of that issue for days and weeks to come. I somehow had to figure out a way to make Jackie Dee mine, and what I mean by that was to marry her if she would even have me.

I hadn't even proposed to her yet, and we had only been back together for about a month now, yet all I could think about from that night on was marrying Jackie Dee. I wanted so much to believe that the two of us coming together that night had forever consummated and sealed our relationship, but had it really? In every sense of the word, I felt that we had truly become one that night, and now we were pretty much inseparable.

Jackie had taken everything from me that night. She took all my love, my heart, and last but not least, my virginity. And what did I get in return? Paradise. Paradise had been restored to me. I was glad to have given it all up on a silver platter to her and only her. There absolutely, positively could not have been any other lover in my life. From that very first day when I saw Jackie Dee smile and I discovered that she was the girl of my dreams, I was all hers for the taking. All Jackie had to do was reach out to me, and she could have had me any time she wanted. Hell, I would have been willing to crawl to her. I heard a line in a song somewhere that went "You had me from hello." Well, Jackie had not even had to speak a word; all she had to do was smile, and she had me from then on.

You know, there is something inside of me even now as I think back and remember that night that will just not let me stop writing about it. Some might call it verbosity, but in reality, I am just being truthful about what took place on that one perfect and most pleasurable night. I know that I was nineteen years old and that it was my first time, but the two of us lying there and loving each other ever so affectionately all night long was the most sensually erotic experience of my entire life. Never in my wildest dreams had I ever imagined that the two of us coming together would culminate into such an exotic adventure as that night had.

In fact, from this night on, the sexual chemistry that existed between Jackie and me was nothing short of phenomenal. In a manner of speaking, what was once unexplored territory—had now been surveyed, mapped, and charted; the treasure chest too having been discovered, opened and plundered. We got so carried away with loving each other that night that it felt like we were transported out of my bedroom and onto some higher plane in paradise where only a handful of true lovers had gone before us: Adam and Eve, Mark Antony and Cleopatra, Romeo and Juliet, and now Jackie and Daniel. I know you're probably think I'm getting carried away here, but true, genuine love has away of making you do just that.

Now, I know that Romeo and Juliet were from a Shakespearian play, but I find it ironic that Juliet was as young as twelve years old when she fell in love with Romeo and thirteen when Friar Lawrence married them. Sometimes love just doesn't make any sense or follow any course of logic or any set of rules. For couples who are truly in love, depending on their level of commitment to each other, I believe that love makes its own sets of rules. It conforms, shapes, and fashions itself around the couples who have truly fallen helplessly into its grasp. My heart goes out to those who have yet to experience the kind of love that I'm talking about. However, I believe that there is someone out there just for you and only you; so the two of you can explore and discover the breadth, length, depth, and height of the magic that is in the kind of romantic love I'm writing about here. Thank God that I found the only lover who could have ever satisfied me at an early age, and I did not have to look any farther than across the street to find the girl of my dreams.

My experiences concerning the pursuit of true love are as follows:

It will have you up and pacing the floor at all hours of the night.

It will have you down on your knees begging or crawling across the front lawn.

It will have you so turned around that you won't know if you are coming or going.

You won't know whether to sit, stand, or kneel.

It will take you places you didn't want to go.

It will leave you there longer than you wanted to stay.

And yes, it will have you talking to yourself—believe me, I know.

True love is like a many-faceted diamond. Each time you look at it from a different angle, you see a different glimmer of its beauty. And that's the kind of love that I have had all along for Jackie Dee, since I first saw her smile. Each time I take Jackie into my arms and look into those hazel-colored eyes, each time her lips touch mine; I'm transported to another plateau in paradise that I have yet to explore. And the only reason I can share these precious thoughts that are pouring out of my heart with you is that on one hot, summer's day more than thirty-five years ago, I saw a little girl smile. Just like that, *the eyes of my heart were forever opened.* I believe for the purpose of experiencing truelove in a real and genuine way with the girl of my dreams.

It is because of my ever-increasing love for Jackie Dee that these heartfelt emotions still exist within me, and it is because of her love for me that these heartfelt emotions can surface. I have heard that love is like oxygen and that if you get too much of it, it makes you high. Well, if that is the case, then anytime I was ever with Jackie Dee, I most definitely was stoned out of my ever-loving mind.

You know how you can tell when two people are really in love? Let me give you an example. On that truly extraordinary night when the two of us came together for the first time, we were already lamenting the fact that twelve hours from then, she would have to go back home and that it would be another three or fours hours before we would see each other again. Twelve hours from then—is that ridiculous or what? No, that is just two young lovers lost in each other's love.

I have never heard, seen, or read anything about this kind of love that I have for Jackie Dee. I would bet that this kind of love, the love I have for her, only comes around once every trillion years. You can't eat, you can't sleep, and you can't keep a clear head to think about anything else. It's been more than thirty-five years now, and I'm still just as much in love with Jackie Dee today as I was back on that first day I saw her smile. This is just one of the reasons why I feel the need to record my testimony. In addition, I want to share with everyone how blessed I was—yet at the same time somewhat cursed—with this love I have for her. It is like receiving the greatest news of your life; you cannot help it, you just have to share it with somebody by shouting it out at the top of your lungs! What possible good could come of keeping the greatest experience that has ever graced your life all to yourself?

I shudder to think that if I had allowed my life to slip away just weeks before, I never would have tasted and experienced another facet of paradise—in making love to Jackie Dee. That truly would have been a god-awful tragedy.

For me, on that night, the eternal question that has plagued mankind since the beginning of time was answered. Yes—God does exist. It was just that incredible.

Anyway, the following morning came, and Jackie had to get up and get ready to make her journey all the way back home … across the street. We could hardly tear ourselves apart long enough to do anything that morning. It was like we were joined at the hip or something. We just couldn't let go of one another after all that had happened just a few hours earlier. What a fantastic night filled with such intense passion and pleasure the two of us had together!

Jackie went home without incident that day, and we met back up at her friend Penny's house just a few hours later. Nevertheless, the anticipation leading up to seeing Jackie again was simply unbearable. I was naive, and I thought her parents would somehow be able to tell what Jackie and I had done the night before. I thought they would be able to see some kind of evidence of it on her. After all, it was my first time, so I just didn't know what to expect.

During that period of time, Jackie and I had to be really creative in figuring out ways we could see each other without her parents finding out.

One of our favorite little deceptions was for Jackie to tell her mom she was babysitting my baby brother. Then I would telephone a cab and instruct them to pick me up in front of my house. When her folks saw the cab pull up in front, they would send Jackie over to baby-sit my brother for the night.

Once I was inside the cab, I would tell the cabbie to drive halfway around to the next block. Then I would toss him five bucks and get out of the car. I would cut through the backyard adjacent to mine and go through my back door, and hello, Jackie Dee!

We kept this up every Friday night and some Saturday nights all summer long, and damn, those were the days. Jackie and I had some earthshaking times together on those long, hot summer nights. We had to keep up little deceptions like this as well as other clandestine schemes just so we could see each other.

One Friday afternoon in early August, Jackie called me up to tell me that she and her family were taking a drive down to her grandma Maxine's farm in Stover, Missouri. Before she left, though, she wanted to give me a letter that she had written for me. I met Jackie out in front of my house. We embraced and kissed each other, and she passed me the letter. She asked me to read it later when I began to miss her. She said she had to go just then because everyone was waiting for her. Within moments after that, Jackie and her parents had barely left the house and before they could even back out of their driveway, I began to miss her already. Is that awful or what?

Shortly after Jackie left that day, I received a call from someone whom I really didn't know that well. His name was Chuck, and I was puzzled by how he knew my phone number. When I asked him, he could not give me a straight answer. But I remembered that I'd met him at a party once and that he seemed okay.

Chuck was calling to invite me to a party that was taking place that night on the other side of town. With Jackie gone for the weekend, I thought, "What the hell" and accepted his invitation. With Jackie's note folded and stuffed in my back pocket, I headed out the door and drove across town.

When I arrived, I began mingling with some folks who had already begun partying. I noticed very quickly that I hardly knew anyone there besides Chuck. I also noticed something else. Every time I turned around, someone was handing me a beer to drink. There were all kinds of strong drinks, marijuana, and other drugs at this party.

The party started off innocently enough. Then most of the guys there decided that they wanted to have an arm-wrestling match. I knew from previous party experiences that these kinds of contests never ended amicably. The arm-wrestling contest quickly escalated into a chest-boxing match, and before the night was over, I ended up punching one guy in the jaw and another one in the ear.

As if that weren't bad enough already, there was this gal named Donna at the party who was trying to come on to me the whole time. And to make matters worse, she was married. I did what I could to ignore her, and I think her husband must have been intimidated by me because he did not say or do a thing to stop her flirtatious behavior.

As the night wore on, I felt the crowd beginning to get a little hostile towards me. It felt like the walls were closing in around me. To make matters worse, I was beginning to feel the effects of all the alcohol I had drunk that night, which was quite a lot. For me, the night had all the ingredients for disaster.

I noticed that the only person I sort of knew—Chuck, the one who had invited me to the party—was nowhere in sight. I mean, he was gone. Something was terribly wrong with me, but what was it? I went into the kitchen and sat at the table alone, trying for the life of me to compose myself, but I could not.

Then it hit me; I had been drugged. I also realized something else; I had forgotten my gun and left it at home. I thought what an idiot I must be. I could feel the effects of the drug spreading rapidly through my body, and even the easiest of tasks became quite difficult for me to manage. I knew that if I did not make an immediate effort to escape from this hostile crowd, there was a good chance that I would be at their mercy and unable to defend myself.

I saw a telephone there on the wall of the kitchen, but due to the effects of the drug, I couldn't remember any phone numbers; that is in the right sequence anyway. I also noticed an open window, so I rose to my feet and stumbled over to it. I sat down on the windowsill and purposefully fell over backwards out of the window. It was the only thing I could manage to do at the time. The drop from the window to the ground was only about a five or six-feet.

The fall to the ground and the night air helped to revive me, but only momentarily. I managed to get to my feet and started walking between the houses and down the street. I had made it about a block and a half away when I heard footsteps quickly approaching me. As I turned to see who it was, I was met with a crushing blow to the head with what felt like a ball-bat, and down I went.

The last thing I remember is lying there on the sidewalk and being kicked in the head and face repeatedly. I could see what looked like flashbulbs going off before my eyes, and there were sharp, ear-piercing, shrill sounds in my ears. I subsequently lost consciousness.

Some time later, I began to come out of it, and I could feel the cool grass against my face. I was lying face down on the ground. With each passing second, I revived more and more, and each part of my body began to shrug off the after-effects of the drugs, the alcohol, and the beating. My right eye was swollen shut, but I could see plainly out of the other one. I was still barely able to move.

As I looked around, I could see that I was back at the house where I'd been partying earlier. Apparently, the guys who had jumped me had dragged me all the way back to the house and dumped me in the front yard. From where I lay, I could see the guys and Donna on the front porch of the house, but I could not hear a sound. Their mouths were moving, but there were no audible sounds. It was just plain weird.

One of these guys came off the front porch, started kicking me in the ribs, and then began pouring vodka all over me. I could not do anything but lie there and take it. I eventually passed out again. When I came to, my hearing was back, and I could hear them all talking. As I continued to slip in and out of consciousness, I thought I could hear them saying things like "Let's dump him in the river or run over him with the car." I knew I had better do something quick, but what? I was still very much out of it, and I was not quite sure what I could do at that point.

Just then, Donna came off the porch and straddled me as I lay face down on the grass. She lifted my head off the ground by my long hair, pulling it all the way back. Then she took her thumb and pressed it against my neck, sliding it back and forth in a cutthroat-like fashion. I heard her say, "I'm going to go get a knife and do this guy for real."

As she was getting off of me, she reached into my back pocket and took out the note Jackie had written me before leaving for the farm earlier that day. I thought, "My God, will I ever see my Jackie Dee again?" Then I thought, "Come on, you lazy bastard—do something."

While Donna was opening the note that Jackie had written me, I began to try to move my legs and arms around to see if anything was broken. Everything seemed to be working fine except that there was a pounding sensation in my head. Donna began reading the note, which I had not had a chance to read myself, and something came over me in that moment. I became so enraged that I was on the verge of going absolutely berserk.

Donna read, "From Jackie Stone—I know that bitch!" She continued reading the note and said, "Oh, she loves you, huh? Oh, she promises never to leave you—"

Just then, with every ounce of energy I could muster, I jumped to my feet. You should have seen the look on Donna's face; her jaw dropped wide open in utter disbelief, as I was now standing over her—probably looking like something out of a horror flick. I grabbed a handful of her hair and twisted it around my left hand, and yes, I clobbered this girl with an overhand right. I snatched the note from her hand as she went sprawling backwards and onto the ground.

The guys up on the porch heard the thud, looked around, and noticed what I had just done. One of them yelled, "He's up—get him!"

I took off and ran as fast as I could, probably faster than I had ever run before. I dodged between houses and jumped over cars, fences, and anything else that stood in my way of escaping from those guys. As I was running, I thought to myself, "If I'm fortunate enough to survive this night, I'm going to come back here and kill every last one of these motherfuckers if it's the last thing I do."

I hurdled a last fence and then burrowed myself down into some leaves and lay very still. I could hear dogs barking throughout the neighborhood, and the guys who were chasing me were close by, yelling, "He's over here!" "No, he's over here!"

Just then, I heard someone who lived in one of the houses yell, "Get off of my property, or I'll blow your heads off!"

Another person from the house next-door yelled, "Get out of here! I'll teach you to trespass on my property—I'm calling the cops!"

I continued lying there until I eventually passed out again from the pounding in my head. When I came to, I wasn't sure if I had given my attackers the slip or if they were still standing close by. I tried not to make a sound by accidentally rustling the leaves that covered me. But the only sound I could hear was the wind blowing through the leaves on the tree.

Still feeling the after-effects of the drug, I rose to my feet, shook the leaves off of me, and headed for home as the night began to give way to the light of day. Once I was home, I collapsed on my bed and passed out. I did not wake up for two whole days. Finally, the girl of my dreams, Jackie Dee, awakened me. As she rolled me over in my bed, she began crying in horror; she could not believe the extent of the injuries to my face and head. It looked like one big, continuous scab was covering the entire right side of my face and head. There was still some swelling and discomfort to my head. Jackie insisted that I go to the hospital, but I asked her to doctor me up instead. Jackie agreed, and she did an excellent job of tending to my wounds and nursing me back to health. Her bedside manner was just what any doctor would have ordered. I told Jackie about everything that had happened to me as she sat there consoling me while holding my hand.

Unbelievably, Jackie and I found out a few days later that the whole attack that night had been a set-up. Apparently, it was all due to a falling out that Jackie and I had had with Billy; he was the one who had set me up that night. You may remember that Billy had been a friend of mine whom Jackie had liked at one time. He was the guy I used to punch and knock around a year or two earlier. This was that same Billy who had tried to pick up the girls at the drive-in on my eighteenth birthday, then wouldn't even get out of the car to help me when those guys were kicking the shit out of me.

The whole thing had started a couple of weeks before when Billy had slapped Jackie because she refused his advances. Jackie delayed telling me about the incident for fear of what I might do to him, but then she finally told me what he had done. Once I knew what had happened, I went looking for Billy, but I could not find him for days. I thought that maybe he had moved out of the area because nobody knew where he was. My theory is that Billy was jealous of Jackie and me. I think he knew that I would come looking for him for slapping Jackie, so he devised a scheme to have his friends take the wind out of my sails, so to speak. I hadn't even done anything to him yet.

Billy had asked Chuck, whom I hardly knew, to invite me to this party where he'd had the other guys, whom I didn't know either, standing by to jump me and rough me up a bit. The part about drugging me up was just an afterthought—they'd thought it would help them slow me down. That explained why every time I had turned around that night, someone was offering me a beer.

Jackie and I found all this out because shortly after that night I was jumped, when I had recovered enough to rumble again, I went back down to the house where it had all taken place.

I took my close friend John, who had joined the Marines, but was home on leave, and another friend of mine named Craig, who was home on leave from the Navy. After the three of us drove down there, we ran up onto the front porch, and rather than knocking on the front door, I grabbed a heavy steel lawn chair from the front porch and threw it through a huge, plate-glass window on the front of the house. Then we jumped through the window and started kicking the shit out of everybody inside.

One of the guys who was in the house that day was Chuck. I had him pinned behind a sofa and was punching him in the face when he began telling me about the set-up and who was ultimately responsible for it.

It all made sense to me now, so after exacting the amount of pain and suffering I had endured on those guys, we left there and went looking for Billy, who was responsible for the whole melee. We drove all over town looking for him, but we could not find him anywhere. No one seemed to know where he was.

Just then, I remembered that Billy had a brother name Jerry, and I knew where Jerry worked. We went down to Jerry's place of employment, and I asked him straight up where his brother Billy was hiding. Jerry said, "I figured you would eventually find your way to me, but I didn't have anything to do with what those guys did to you. I just heard about it after it all went down."

Jerry went on to say that Billy was no longer in town; he had moved back home, which was out of the state. I told Jerry to tell his brother that it made no difference to me whether he had moved out of the state or out of the country; he had better get used to looking over his shoulder, because I was coming after him regardless of where he was hiding, and I would eventually find him. As it turned out, Jerry was telling the truth, and it would be months before I would see Billy again, as you will see.

It was now mid-August, and Jackie and I were hanging out together at my place one evening. That night, her step-dad Paul got wise and tried hanging out in my next-door neighbor's backyard to see if he could spot Jackie coming out of my back door. She was supposed to be at her friend Penny's house that evening, but Jackie's parents had already gone over to Penny's earlier to see if she was really there. Of course she wasn't, because she was with me at my place.

From my darkened bedroom window, I spotted Paul sitting in my neighbor's backyard. I had him scoped out in my sights with my rifle and at the very least wanted to shoot over his head to scare the shit out of him, but Jackie begged me not to. So I called the police instead and told them there was a peeping

Tom in my neighbor's backyard trying to look into his rear window. The police came with dogs, guns, and flashlights. It was quite a spectacle to behold, watching Paul try to explain to the cops what the hell he was doing in my neighbor's backyard.

Needless to say, Jackie and I both got quite a kick out of that little prank. I was so ornery in those days that later that night, I poured some sugar down the gas tank of his vehicle. I just couldn't help myself, really.

Anyway, while the police were more than likely handcuffing Paul out in front, we slipped out the back door and through the yard, walked over onto Poplar, and headed for Penny's house. Her place had turned into our second-favorite place to rendezvous after my place. Penny's house was also a regular partying house for Jackie, me and some of the other neighborhood teenagers. Penny's mother never stopped us from doing pretty much whatever we wanted so long as I brought her a bottle of Southern Comfort (eighty proof) whiskey. Mary would retire to her bedroom with it, and we would not see her for the rest of the night no matter how loud we or the music got.

Not long after that, Jackie's parents arranged for her to go visit some relatives in Georgia, probably to get her away from me. Jackie had been gone now for what seemed like a month—though it was actually only about two weeks—when my telephone rang. It was the Georgia phone operator asking me if I would accept a collect call from a Jackie Dee Stone.

I said, "You bet your ass I will."

Jackie's voice came over the telephone, and we talked for about fifteen minutes about how much we missed seeing each other and what we planned to do together when she returned home from Georgia. We also talked about what each of us had been up to since we had last seen one another, and then Jackie said she had to go. We said our good-byes, and then she hung up.

A few minutes later, I heard a knock at my back door. I went to answer the door, and it was none other than Jackie Dee! How could it be Jackie when she was in Georgia? I thought I was dreaming or hallucinating again. But here's what had really happened: Jackie's mom was pretending to be the Georgia telephone operator, and Jackie had been at home across the street all along. She had just arrived home from Georgia that morning, and she and her mother had decided to pull a fast one on me. It worked; I never suspected a thing. I thought a miracle had occurred to bring her back home to me.

Jackie Dee looked absolutely gorgeous that day; her hair had been lightened by the Georgia sunrays, and she was so nice and tan that just looking at her made my mouth water. In those days, I liked to refer to Jackie as my cinnamon girl because she tasted so sweet and always sported a tan.

That day, we got reacquainted and made up for lost time, because we had not seen each other for a couple of weeks now. We had my brother Scott take some pictures of us with the camera I had bought for Jackie on her birthday. I still have the pictures that he took of us that day in my backyard and my front living room. Incidentally, one of those pictures is on the cover of this book.

8

Fighting Against All Odds

That same day that Jackie returned from Georgia, we ended up sitting under a red maple tree in my backyard. I was sitting on the ground with my back up against the tree, and Jackie was sitting between my legs with her back to my chest. I had my arms folded around her waist, and my chin was resting on her shoulder. I said to Jackie, "I wish there was someplace we could go where people would just leave us alone." Then I said, "And when we get married—"

Jackie interrupted me and said, "What did you just say?"

I said, "And when we get married—"

She said, "Get married? When did you decide this, and when were you going to talk to me about it?"

You see, I had never officially proposed to Jackie Dee. Like the fool that I was, I just assumed that Jackie felt the same way about me as I felt about her. In reality, as you read this story was nothing short of an impossibility and was definitely wishful thinking on my part. But in response to Jackie's question, I simply said, "When two people love each other as much as we do, the normal course of events would be for us to get married."

Jackie didn't say yes, and she did not say no, either. She seemed somewhat evasive about the matter, which at the time I thought was because she knew she was too young to marry me at this point in time anyway. Nevertheless, I was feeling pretty confident about where our relationship was headed until one night.

I went with my friend John to collect some money that some guys had borrowed from him. We recovered the money, but we had to knock some guy's teeth out, and we sustained some cuts and bruises ourselves. Before it got too late in the evening, I tried to call Jackie on the telephone to talk to her and to hear the sound of her voice. Jackie's mom answered the phone and said that Jackie was not at home, but she would not tell me where she was or who she was with. I didn't know if her mom was being truthful with me or not; I didn't know what to think.

The next morning, I woke up early hurting from head to toe from fighting and brawling about the night before. I tried calling Jackie again. I had not seen or talked with her for about a day and a half, and that was about all I could stand. Jackie answered the phone, but I could tell immediately from the tone of her voice that something was wrong. She was being somewhat combative and argumentative with me, but I knew there was nothing to argue about. Then Jackie suddenly said that she did not think things were going to work out between the two of us and that she was contemplating breaking up with me.

I asked Jackie, "What the hell has happened to make you change your mind about us so quickly after all that we've been through? Won't you at least tell me? For God's sake, Jackie, please tell me." I asked her if it had anything to do with where she had been the night before.

Jackie said, "What do you mean?"

I said, "I tried to call you last night, but your mother said you were out, and she would not tell me where you were or who you were with."

All Jackie would say was "I just don't think it's going to work out between us," but she would not tell me why. She literally had me in tears, begging her over the telephone to please not do this to me again.

Sharon, who was John's girlfriend, overheard me begging Jackie not to break up with me, and she came into the room. Sharon, seeing that I was visibly distraught and upset—said to me, "Good heavens, Daniel, just let her go."

I put my hand over the phone so that Jackie could not hear us, and I told Sharon that she wouldn't understand. I said, "Believe me, you don't know the hold this girl has on me. I can never let her go—ever." In my mind, I was thinking, "Let the girl of my dreams go; my heart would never allow it, not in a trillion years."

I got back on the phone and told Jackie that I was coming over to discuss things with her and that I would be there in fifteen minutes. I didn't even take the time to put my shirt or my shoes on; I just ran out of John's house and jumped into the car. I drove at breakneck speed all the way over to Jackie's place, running every red light across town, just like I used to do.

On the drive over there, I thought that I was getting exactly what I deserved for falling so deeply and madly in love with someone so young. I mean I had no idea that trying to hold onto my dream was going to be so difficult, but I had lost my heart to her so long ago. Then again, I didn't really have any choice in the matter; it was over for me the first time I saw Jackie Dee smile. What could I possibly do? The only answer I could come up with—was that I had to hold onto my dream the best I possibly could until there was absolutely nothing left for me to hold on to …

Now later that same day, Jackie and I were supposed to go to one of those summer-jam concerts, where multiple rock groups would be performing.

Anyway, I made it to Jackie's house in less than ten minutes. Jackie saw me coming up the walk, and she came out of the house displaying that precious smile of hers. Then she hugged me and kissed me. We sat on her front porch, and when I looked down, I noticed that I was still barefoot.

I didn't know whether her parents were home or not, but I really didn't care at this point in our relationship, and neither did she. I caressed her face and kissed her ear and neck, and I asked her what was going on that had made her even consider breaking up with me again.

Just then, I noticed that there were two large hickeys on the back of her neck. So enraged and tearful that I could not even see straight, I said, "Damn it, what in the fuck is this?"

Jackie said, "You see, that's what I mean."

After some prodding, she finally told me that she had been with her ex-boyfriend Mark the night before, though she would not give me any details about what the two of them had been doing together. I got the sense that whatever had taken place between the two of them was consensual, so I had no choice but to imagine how he had positioned himself to get those hickeys way back there. I could see that Jackie was becoming visibly upset with me. Probably because I had found those hickeys on the back of her neck so quickly that was supposed to be hidden.

For that reason, and due to the fact that not even half an hour before, she had been talking about breaking up with me. I knew at that moment as I sat next to Jackie on her front porch, that if I were to have any chance of continuing to see her, I had to drop the matter entirely. I forced myself to do so, even though I was utterly devastated that she would allow that shit-ass to even touch her again, let alone put his damn mouth on her neck. But as hard as it was for me to do, I showed great restraint and swallowed my pride, choking on it as it went down my throat. No matter how much it hurt and caused my heart to ache, I had to let it go and pretend it had never happened.

One time before this incident, I saw Mark's car parked out in front of Jackie's house, so I went over there and knocked on the door. When Jackie answered it, I asked her, "What the hell is he doing here? Tell that little piss ant to come outside for a minute." Believe me, a New York minute is all I would have needed to make quick work of that prick-shit. But she would not. Instead, she would say, "Please don't cause any trouble."

Jackie told me that on occasion, her mom asked Mark to come over and work on one thing or another in the house. That particular time, he was supposedly there to work on the dryer.

I know now that this wasn't the truth; that idiot couldn't change a flat tire if his life depended on it, let alone work on a dryer. I found this out some years later when Mark implored me to help him change his car battery.

Because when he tried to jump-start his car from a passerby, the dope crossed the positive terminal with the negative and blew the car battery up in his face. While I was changing the battery for him, I couldn't help but notice that he had a flat tire, too. I found out that day that he didn't even know how to work a four-way tire tool, let alone change a flat.

It seemed like whenever I was on the cusp of sharing some-thing special, and in depth from my heart with Jackie Dee, things like this would happen and cause me to become suspicious about whether she really loved me at all. In contrast, it would subsequently keep me from sharing my innermost feelings with Jackie. Furthermore, it made me suppress them even deeper inside my heart.

Just when I thought I might be able to relax and feel good about my and Jackie's relationship, then something would go wrong. Every now and then, incidents like this one would cause me to just take off and go work off some steam. On other occasions, I would drink rather heavily to help me cope with my anger, frustrations, doubts, suspicions, and lack of self-worth; I mean all of it.

Anyway, later that same day, Jackie and I went to the concert with my brother and his girlfriend, but I could not enjoy the show because I was still thinking about what had taken place that morning. I was still very angry and upset, but for the life of me, I had to conceal my anger even though I could feel my heart breaking apart inside me. I could not sit still, but I had to pretend I was having a good time and that everything was okay.

In between stage performances, my brother and his girlfriend got up to use the restrooms, and Jackie said she needed to go use the restroom too. Just then, I thought I saw the person who was sitting behind Jackie jerk, and it looked like his foot kicked the back of her head. I jumped up as Jackie was getting out of her seat and asked, "Did he just kick you?"

She said, "I think so, I thought I felt something nudge me back there." You have to remember that this was at a rock concert in the summer of 1977, and quite a bit of stuff was being passed around, if you know what I mean.

They all left to go to the restroom, and I told them I would stay behind to watch our seats and belongings. We had all bought T-shirts and stuff when we'd first arrived at the concert.

Now, the man who had kicked Jackie had had way too much to drink; he had already been drinking when he and his friends had first arrived. When Jackie, my brother, and his girlfriend were out of sight, I climbed over into the row of seats behind me and asked the two individuals sitting on either side of this man, "Is he with either of you?"

They said, "No, he is not."

So I yelled at the man, "You son of a bitch!" Then I swung and struck the guy in the left eye with my fist. In all honesty, I didn't care if he had kicked Jackie inadvertently or not; I just wanted to hit him for even touching her. I hit him so hard that he had an instant black eye and was out cold like a dead man. I climbed back into my seat, and out of the corner of my eye, I saw the people behind me pick the guy up, one under each shoulder, and drag him off. They didn't return to their seats for the rest of the concert.

When Jackie, my brother, and his girlfriend returned, they said, "Where are the guys who were sitting behind us?"

I said, "I guess they didn't like the show and left." I felt a little better for having worked off some steam, but it wasn't nearly enough, not by a long shot.

Later that same weekend, I received a phone call from my friend John. He called to inform me that another friend of mine was back in town. Yup—it was Billy, the guy who had set me up the night that those guys had drugged me and gave me a pretty good working over. John went on to say that he had taken the liberty of inviting Billy to a party that a mutual acquaintance of ours was throwing that night.

John said, "I'll tell you, Daniel, before Billy would commit to coming to the party, he asked me if you were going to be there. So I told him no, and that you didn't know anything about it."

I told John thanks for setting that up and that I really appreciated it. I owed Billy a lot of pain, and that this was just what I needed, especially in light of everything else that had happened that weekend.

I showed up at the party early, and John suggested that I hide behind the bar for "if and when" Billy showed up. He said, "When you hear me whistle, then you can jump out from behind the bar and punch the guy's lights out."

I said, "That sounds great; let's do it."

Shortly thereafter, Billy arrived, and I hid behind the bar as planned and waited for John to give me the signal. Billy, oblivious to what was about to occur, began looking around the place to see who was there. Just when he thought it was safe to take a seat in this rocking chair, John began whistling. I came out from behind the bar and walked up behind Billy, the person who was responsible for setting me up that night. The night I had to endure such humiliation, such embarrassment, and a pretty good working over I might add, that I wasn't going to forget about it anytime soon. However, of even greater importance was how it had all gotten started—and that was due to the fact that Billy had slapped the girl of my dreams, Jackie Dee. For that reason, today was his day of reckoning; it was payback time for that son of a bitch. Billy was one of the last ones on a long list of assholes that I had placed on my personal shit list for retribution purposes.

Billy sat there, totally unaware of what was about to unfold, and continued rocking in the rocking chair. I started to move around in front of him, when he saw me out of the corner of his eye. You should have seen the look that came over Billy's face—he looked as though someone had just walked over his grave, and his face turned white as a ghost. He began to tremble and shake.

Stuttering and stammering, Billy said, "Daniel, what are you doing here?"

I said, "Why, I've come here to see you, Billy."

I told Billy to stand up, but he would not. So I hollered at him, "If you ever lay a hand on Jackie again, I will kill you, your whole family, your pets, plants—everything wasted, you motherfucker!" I spat in Billy's face, and then I punched the son of a bitch back to the Stone Age. While I was punching away at Billy, the right arm of the rocking chair he was sitting in broke off as he and it hit the floor. As Billy lay on the floor, I noticed that he wasn't moving, and I was far from being finished with that piece of shit. I had not even begun to exact the measure of pain I had in store for him.

I told my friends to stand Billy up, but he was too limp and hard to handle. I began to slap and backhand him across the face to revive him, but he was out cold. I could see the left side of his face beginning to swell up, and his left eye was turning black. We threw him into one of the spare rooms that was situated off the main room we all were in until he woke up.

Later on, one of my friends went to check on Billy in the other room. My friend called to us to come quickly, so we did. When we looked around the room, we saw that Billy was gone. Apparently, he had escaped through the open window. Shit!

After that night, I never saw Billy's face again. He had left town for good.

It was now the end of August, and school was about to start back up. It was around this time that Jackie's parents began grounding her, forbidding her to leave the house more frequently now. In addition to this, they would not allow Jackie to talk to me over the telephone, making it extremely difficult for us to maintain our relationship. If Jackie could manage to stay out of trouble for a week, then they would occasionally let her spend the night with her friend Penny.

One of these times that Jackie spent the night with Penny, she made up her mind that she'd had enough of her parents preventing her from having anything to do with me. She decided not to return home the next day, or the next day, or the day after that.

Her parents called the police, the neighbors, and the local radio station. They even got her ex-boyfriend Mark and his mentally challenged uncle, a wannabe cop, involved in the search. But Jackie and I were always one step ahead of them all. While the police were searching Penny's house, Jackie would be at my house. While the police were searching my house, Jackie and I would be back at Penny's house. If we saw anyone who looked suspicious coming toward my house or Penny's house, we would just head out the back door and then come back later.

Jackie's parents called my mom and threatened to have me thrown in jail if I did not reveal where Jackie Dee was hiding out. Obviously, my response to all of this was "Screw 'em, screw 'em all!" This was the girl of my dreams they were trying to take away from me again.

Jackie eventually returned home after talking things over with her mother on the phone. They worked out some kind of compromise in which her parents would back off a little in controlling what she could and could not do.

One night while Jackie and I were out on a date, driving around on my suspended driver's license, a policeman saw me speeding down 23rd Street. The policeman began to give chase, and I turned down one road after another, trying to lose him. I knew that if he were to catch us, there was a good chance that I would be arrested and that Jackie would have to walk home from that area. And I was not about to let that happen. It was even worse of an area than the one we lived in, if that was even possible. Jackie began to cry; she was more afraid of me going to jail than she was of the policeman that was chasing us. Even though it hurt me to see Jackie cry, her tears expressed genuine concern for me, and that she did care about me. In Jackie's tears that night, I could feel and see her love for me.

I actually managed to lose the cop for a few minutes. When he was nowhere in sight, I turned right down this one side road. But as chance would have it, the patrolman happened to be crossing the intersection we had just passed, and that's when he spotted us. I told Jackie to stuff her purse up under the seat, and to stay in the car no matter what happened. I took my wallet out of my back pocket and threw it and my revolver under the front seat. Then I pulled over, jumped out of the car, and started running back toward the police car, waving my arms. I began shouting, "We've been robbed, we've been robbed!"

The policeman jumped out of his patrol car and said, "Sir, I need you to calm down and explain to me what is going on."

I said, "My girlfriend and I were just robbed."

I went on to say that when we were stopped at a stop sign, a man had approached the vehicle and stuck a gun in my face. He had told me to hand over my wallet and my girlfriend's purse. When I handed them over to him, he took off running down the street, so I started to chase after him.

Just then, as fate would have it, a call came over the police scanner stating that a man had just snatched some lady's purse a couple of blocks away. The policeman continued questioning me about what the man looked like, what was he wearing, and so forth. The policeman started to ask Jackie what she remembered seeing. I told the cop that the thief had approached my side of the car and that Jackie hadn't had a clear view of him. The policeman asked to see my driver's license. I reached for my wallet, knowing that I did not have it on me. Then I acted distressed and told the police officer, "Oh shit, he got my wallet, my driver's license is in my wallet."

As the policeman was taking down Jackie's and my names, addresses, and phone numbers, another call came over the police radio. The dispatcher stated that they had just apprehended the purse-snatcher around the corner and requested that all available units in close proximity please respond to that area.

The policeman said he had to go and that he would be in touch. As Jackie and I got back in the car and drove away, we both let out a deep sigh of relief.

I was relieved that we were able to avoid Jackie having to walk home that night had I been arrested and taken into custody. Not to mention the fact that I could have been cited for operating a motor vehicle without a valid driver's license, as well as a speeding ticket.

Sure enough, the policeman called me up the next day and wanted Jackie and me to come down to the police station and view the suspect they had arrested the night before as well as the items they had recovered. I convinced the policeman that Jackie hadn't seen what the fictitious man I had made up had looked like. They agreed and asked me to come down to the station and take a look at him. A detective showed up at my house to give me a ride downtown. So I went downtown to police headquarters where the line-up was to take place. I decided on my way down there that I was not going to put the finger on any-body.

By the time I arrived, they had everything set up. I viewed the line-up from left to right, up and down just taking my time really and then I said, "No, I don't see the man who robbed us last night."

One of the detectives said, "Are you sure?"

I said, "Yes, I'm sure."

I thought to myself, "Well, hell yes, I'm sure; he never existed in the first place."

When it was over, they said they were through and sent me on my way. I thought, "Boy, what a narrow escape that whole mess had been."

By this time, school had started back up. Just about every morning when Jackie left her house to "go to school," she headed over to Poplar Street. From there, she cut through my neighbor's backyard and my yard and came through my back door. Jackie and I would spend the whole day together while she was supposed to be at school. You might say that she was in school—she was tutoring me in advanced lessons in lovemak-ing, and I was tutoring her in music appreciation and card-play-ing lessons.

During the months of September and October of 1977, our relationship became more cemented and well established than it had ever been before. On some of the days that Jackie played hooky, we would go have breakfast or lunch and drive around, but never near where we lived. My car was out of commission, so I used my brother's car from time to time. Sometimes Jackie and I would drive to the cemetery and make out or play around in the car while listening to the car radio.

One time, Jackie and I were fooling around in my bedroom and was about to get it on, when there was a knock at my back door. My brother came running into the room to answer the door—he thought it was some friends of ours. But in came Jackie's mother, grandmother, aunt, and little sister, and they caught Jackie and me in bed together. I thought, "Oh shit, here we go!"

Jackie and I were both partially dressed, at least from the waist up. Her family started being very melodramatic, pointing their fingers at us and waving their arms, trying to make Jackie feel guilty and ashamed that her little sister had seen us in bed together. Obviously, I had something to say about all of this, and so with my arms folded back behind my head in a relaxed position taking the whole situation in stride. I said, "If it bothers you so much for Jackie's little sister to witness all of this, then why the hell are you all still standing there and allowing her to see us lying in bed together? Well, answer me, damn it!"

All Jackie's mother could say was, "Jackie, I hope you're proud of yourself, lying in bed with him with no clothes on. I hope you're proud of yourself, young lady." I don't think Jackie was very proud right at that moment, but I do know that she was very much in love with me.

I could have said plenty, knowing a little bit about their own personal history, but I felt now wasn't the time. I also knew that two wrongs didn't make a right; just because we knew certain facts concerning their own personal history, it didn't necessarily make what we were doing right either. However, well—you've read our story and how things culminated to this point in time concerning Jackie's and my very special and unique relationship.

Anyway, they made their usual threats and told Jackie to get dressed and come with them. They all stepped outside and waited for Jackie to put on her clothes.

Jackie gave me a kiss, slipped out of bed, and told me not to worry because they were not going to stop her from seeing me. She seemed so very confident about the whole matter, and it reassured me that she was ready to take a stand against anything that would keep us from being together. It was awesome to witness Jackie growing stronger in her resolve with each piece of clothing that she slipped back on. I could see that Jackie was visibly upset that they had interrupted us, as I was too—before we could finish what we had started. Jackie was so upset with them for barging in on us that I honestly thought that she was going to start peeling her clothes back off again and jump back into bed with me. I remember lying there watching Jackie get dressed and wishing there was some way I could marry her and rescue her from all this bullshit.

I don't know what Jackie said to them that day, but I think she told them that if they continued to interfere with her seeing me, she would run away again.

The first week of November came, and my mother sold the house on Chelsea Street that had been in our family for more than fifty years. We moved eight blocks away to Drury Street, which at that point in time was probably for the best.

Jackie was still upset with her family for coming into my bedroom that day, and she was further upset by the fact that we would not be able to see each other as easily now. She decided to essentially move out of her mom's house and stay with her great-grandma Elsie. Jackie's great-grandmother lived across the street from Jackie, just a few houses up from where we used to live on Chelsea. It was there at Elsie's that we started meeting each other at night, and we saw each other during the day at my new house on Drury Street.

Jackie and I had figured out a way of seeing each other where she was now living without anyone knowing. Basically, we used the same ingenious idea that we'd used when Jackie used to come to see me at the old house on Chelsea. Only now, and at nightfall, I would cut through the yard on Poplar Street behind her great-grandmother's backyard. Then I would cut through her backyard and climb up onto the roof of her back porch. Once I was on the roof, I would go through the upstairs window, which Jackie would conveniently leave unlocked and opened for me. This also happened to be where Jackie's new bedroom was. I think you can pretty much imagine what we did from there.

The two of us were truly devious as well as inseparable. We stayed up all night in bed together, making plans about everything from getting married to starting a family. One night, Jackie and I sat up there and devised an elaborate scheme in which I would join the military to learn a trade and gain some skills. I had already talked to an army recruiter about joining the U.S. Army and if it were possible to be stationed at Ft. Leonard Wood in Missouri. The army recruiter assured me in writing that Ft. Leonard Wood would be my permanent duty station until I was ready to move on.

Jackie, on the other hand, would convince her folks that she needed to get away to think about things and get a fresh new start on life while living with her grandma Maxine. Maxine for the most part, lived alone in Stover, MO. Jackie could attend high school there. While Jackie was growing up, she had spent some of her summers working on her grandma Maxine's farm, building houses and pole barns and doing the myriad of other chores that were necessary for keeping up and maintaining a farm.

As Jackie and I continued discussing our scheme that night, we also talked about the fact that growing up on Kansas City's east side with all the riff-raff and crime going on around us. That there just weren't any opportunities that were ever afforded us to where we could better ourselves or our situation—besides my enlisting in the military. In fact, I do not remember anyone ever pointing me toward a better way of life or to greener pastures, so to speak. I honestly don't remember ever receiving words of encouragement from anyone in an attempt to steer me in the right direction.

There were simply no role models for us to look up to or compare ourselves with. At least where we could honestly say, "That's who we want to be like, that's where we want to be so many years from now." There was just no guiding light or voice to help Jackie or me along the way.

As fate would have it, Jackie's folks bought our little scheme hook, line, and sinker and gave their permission for Jackie to move to Stover, MO. Then again, they probably would have consented to any scheme that would put as much distance between her and me as humanly possible. Of course, the only reason Jackie and I had come up with this elaborate plan in the first place was that we always encountered so much resistance when we tried to see each other in Kansas City. We felt like we literally had to get out of town in order to be able to maintain our hot and heavy relationship.

Of course, Jackie's parents didn't know that I was planning on going into the military and being stationed at Ft. Leonard Wood, ninety miles away from Stover. I, on the other hand, knew that I could drive back and forth from Ft. Leonard Wood to Stover to see Jackie Dee on my weekend passes. Jackie's grandfather Harry had a job in Kansas City and drove all the way to Stover on the weekends if he wasn't too tired.

Our plan was in full swing. Jackie made the necessary arrangements to depart for her grandma's farm in Stover, and I joined the U. S. Army, Combat Engineers' Division. On December 4, 1977, I was supposed to report for duty at Ft. Leonard Wood. Midway through November, Jackie withdrew from school in Kansas City, packed her belongings, and headed for Stover. We made plans for me to drive down to Stover a couple of days later, once I had taken care of everything back in Kansas City. That way I could spend two weeks with Jackie at her grandma Maxine's farm before reporting for duty.

Jackie could pretty much talk her grandmother Maxine into letting her do whatever she wanted. She could even smoke cigarettes in front of her grandma.

That week, the camshaft in my motor snapped in two, and there wasn't time for me to repair it. Another car that I was supposed to buy from my brother did not materialize as planned, so I ended up taking the bus down to Sedalia, which was as close as it went to Stover.

Stover and Sedalia are about thirty miles apart. It had been about a week since Jackie Dee and I had seen each other, and the anticipation that welled up inside of me as I waited for Jackie and her grandfather to pick me up at the bus station was almost more than I could bear. Jackie and I had become so attached to one another during the last couple of months that being apart for even a single day drove us crazy. I tried to wait patiently for them, but I just could not sit still and began pacing the floor. Just then, they pulled up in the car. I took one look at

Jackie and got so excited that I became lightheaded and dizzy and thought I was going to pass out.

Jackie Dee looked exceptionally beautiful that night. She had done her facial makeup very nicely, and her long, honey-blonde hair was attractively arranged. The locks of her hair draped over the shoulders of this black, leather jacket she was wearing; thirty years later, I can still remember seeing the way she looked that night. And that smile—oh my God, that smile of hers just does it to me every single time.

I got in the car and sat beside Jackie. I'm telling you, I was about to jump out of my skin with the desire to take her into my arms and kiss her. However, we had to play it cool around her grandparents, so we just held each other's hands ever so tightly all the way back to the farm until later that night ...

While we were at the farm, Jackie and I would often go for long walks in the woods so that we could have some time to ourselves. To put it another way, we went for quite a few long walks down those backcountry roads and hidden grassy paths of Stover, Missouri. On occasion, Jackie's grandma Maxine would drive into town for provisions, which was a ten-mile round trip. Those times also allowed Jackie and me time to ourselves, and believe me; we made the most of it.

Inevitably, the day came when I had to report for duty at Ft. Leonard Wood. Saying good-bye to Jackie Dee, the girl of my dreams, was one of the most difficult things I have ever had to do.

I felt so much more comfortable with Jackie Dee in Stover then back on the east side of Kansas City, where her family and friends could possibly influence her to try to break us up again. I know it sounds like I'm being paranoid, but if you had seen what I saw and gone through what I had experienced, you would fight to hold onto your dreams at all costs too. I was not going to be denied Jackie Dee's presence in my life ever again.

I reported for duty and was sworn in to defend my country. I played the game that was required of me and did whatever it took to earn my weekend pass and see my Jackie Dee. Every weekend, I would hitchhike the ninety miles from Ft. Leonard Wood to Stover. I often ended up walking most of the way, sometimes in sub-zero temperatures, but it wouldn't have mattered if I'd had to walk nine thousand miles. I knew that Jackie Dee, the only pleasant dream I'd ever had, was waiting for me in Stover.

That December, I was awarded a two-week furlough to spend Christmas, New Year's Eve, and New Year's Day with Jackie and her grandma Maxine. It was Jackie Dee's and my first Christmas together, and we were so thankful just to be with each other that we made every second count twice. It was extremely cold outside that Christmas and New Year's. We had a lot of snowfall over the holidays, and so we stayed indoors quite a bit. There was nothing cozier than snuggling up with Jackie Dee on a cold winter's night right there on her grandma's living room floor. Between the two us, we generated enough body heat to melt a two-story igloo with a full basement.

Jackie and I talked to each other over the telephone every day while I was in boot camp and advanced individualized training at Ft. Leonard Wood. When it was not possible for us to talk on the phone, Jackie and I wrote letters to each other, and then the weekends finally came when we could see each other and go for our long walks.

When I tried to sleep at Ft. Leonard Wood, I remember having reoccurring nightmares of losing Jackie Dee all over again. The only thing that seemed to help me sleep more soundly was to have a few beers before going to bed. I often drank beer in the evenings to help me get through the week, but soon I began to drink rather heavily again, since there really wasn't anything else to do. The army had strict guidelines against fighting with fellow military personnel on post, but it did not say anything about fighting in the parks. Brawling, working out in the gym, and long-distance running all helped me to work off some of my anger and frustration of being away from Jackie, as well as some other things that were haunting me from my past. On the weekends, I would make my journey to see Jackie like clockwork. I also sent my monthly paychecks to her, since the army provided me with all the provisions I needed.

While I was going through the civilian side of my training, I was able to take some courses in business administration, theology, and psychology. I actually did very well, and it began to look like some doors were going to open up for me, but nothing ever quite seemed to pan out. In addition, on the military side of my training, the army trained me in combat engineering, demolitions, high-voltage cable splicing, and auto mechanics.

During one of our grenade training exercises, a sergeant was demonstrating the proper way to pull the fuse pin out of a grenade and throw it with one of the young recruits. They were in the bunker next to me when the young recruit pulled the fuse pin out of the grenade, and then accidentally dropped the grenade on the ground. The last thing I remember is the sergeant yelling out "Live grenade!" When I heard that, I attempted to dive to the ground and cover my head.

I woke up in the hospital two days later with a concussion, some loss of hearing in both ears, and a terrible, throbbing headache. The sergeant had survived, but the young recruit had not. I had to stay in the hospital for almost two weeks, which meant that I did not get to see or talk to Jackie Dee for a good portion of that time.

I wanted to see Jackie so very much, and it was driving me crazy just lying there in that hospital bed in recovery. It was the longest time that Jackie and I had been apart since we had gotten back together again.

Finally, I was released from the hospital. The weekend soon arrived, so I began to make my journey to Stover to see Jackie Dee. As usual, I ended up walking for most of it. At one point, I was hitchhiking on a stretch of highway between Iberia and Tuscumbia. This man in an old brown, '65 Buick pulled over and asked me where I was headed. I made it a rule never to tell anyone exactly where I was going, so I responded by saying, "I'm just going up the road a ways."

The man offered me a ride. I got in and said, "My name is Daniel, what's your name?"

He said, "Just call me Mr. Wonderful, everybody does."

I thought, whatever. I was just thankful to finally get off my feet. I was completely exhausted from walking that day, and I was feeling kind of weak from my stay in the hospital. I asked him if I could take my boots off because my feet were burning and aching.

He said, "Sure, kick back and relax."

I took my boots off, and he and I talked about everything from growing up on a farm to military life. I lit up a cigarette and started smoking it, and I offered him one as well. To my surprise, he pulled a joint out of his shirt pocket and said, "I hope you don't mind if I smoke my own brand of cigarettes." He kept offering me a hit, but I refused because of the adverse effects marijuana would have on me as far as my temper was concerned. He continued to pressure me about it, so I finally said, "Okay, let me see what you've got here."

He passed me this little piss ant of a joint, and I started smoking it. As we continued driving up Highway 17, he began to slow down, and then he took a left turn onto some rural road. I said, "Whoa, whoa, wait a minute, what do you think you're doing, man?"

He said, "Relax, I need to take a leak."

As we continued down this road, he suddenly started asking me if I thought he was nice-looking. I said, "What the hell are you talking about? What are you—some kind of fag?"

Just then, he put his hand on my leg. I said, "I'm only going to ask you this one time—get your fucking hand off my leg!"

As he withdrew his hand from my leg, he said, "Man, you just need to calm down, sit back, relax, and go with it."

I said, "Go with it? Why don't you go with this!"

I took my left foot and stomped down on his foot, which was on the gas pedal causing the car to accelerate. Then I turned my upper body to the right and swung my left elbow back, nailing this faggot right in his face. I quickly grabbed the steering wheel and yanked it all the way over to the right, causing the car to turn sideways and go up on two wheels, as we went skidding down the road. The car almost flipped completely over, but then it slammed back down onto all four wheels, stalling the motor out. The car coasted off the road and into an open field before coming to a complete stop.

By this time, I had Mr. Wonderful by the hair and was bashing his face against the steering wheel. He was out cold, bleeding from all over his face like a stuck pig. I threw his coat over his face so I wouldn't have to look at him while I put my boots back on. As I sat there tying my bootlaces, I said to him, "I hope that was as good for you as it was for me."

He began to stir and wake up. I grabbed the car keys out of the ignition and threw them as far as I could into a grassy field. Then I grabbed my gear and began walking down the road all the way back to the main highway. I had run into some unsavory characters in my time hitchhiking along the back roads of Missouri, but none was more unsavory than Mr. Wonderful.

When I finally arrived at the farm, I was so excited to see Jackie that tears literally formed in my eyes.

I was so happy just to be near her again that I could hardly contain myself any time we were alone in the same room. Every time I was with Jackie Dee, I felt like I was home again. My God, that is exactly what true love is supposed to feel like. Just being in her presence and seeing her warm, loving smile made me feel so very fortunate to have her as my girlfriend. I was so attracted to Jackie Dee and so head-over-heels in love with her that all I could think about was marrying her right there on the spot.

I told Jackie and her grandmother about my little encounter with Mr. Wonderful on the highway. I also told them that I didn't think he would be picking anybody else up any time soon, provided he had learned his lesson.

I was still feeling a little weak and tired after my journey and from all that I had been through that week. We all finished watching some late-night television and decided to retire for the night to get some much-needed rest.

About two or three in the morning, I heard my bedroom door open. It was Jackie. She came tiptoeing into the room where I was sleeping that night. Then she slipped into bed and under the covers with me. We started out innocently enough just holding each other, but once again—that soon gave way to an all-out display of emotional fireworks, to the extent that it made this night into one of those special kind of nights that her and I would never ever want to forget. Wow—it was just that incredible. I would like to share more concerning that night, but I think I had better not. Needless to say, neither of us got a wink of sleep that night.

When I returned to Ft. Leonard Wood that following Monday, the drill instructors had our company line up for a field inspection before our twenty-five mile speed-march. My first sergeant conducted his inspection as usual until he got to me. He was looking my weapon and me over when all of a sudden, he yelled, "Good heavens, Private Gutridge—what the hell is that I see on your neck, soldier?"

Before I could answer, he got right up in my face, the brim of his hat just under the brim of my hat, as we stood there eye to eye with his nose almost touching mine until I snapped back, "Drill Sergeant, those are love bites!"

He yelled out, "Love what?"

I yelled back, "They are love bites, Drill Sergeant!"

He said, "They look just like old-fashioned fucking hickeys to me, and I count no fewer than seven of these old-fashioned fucking hickeys!"

I yelled back, "I beg to differ, Drill Sergeant! Those are in fact love bites from my one and only, and they are not—fuck-ing—hickeys!"

He yelled at me once again, "Did you know that I can have your one and only arrested for defacing government property, Private Gutridge?"

I replied, "Drill Sergeant, does that mean that my one and only would get to come down here so that I might possibly be able to get another love bite or two from her?"

The drill sergeant actually busted a gut laughing; it seemed that I must have hit his funny bone with my response. Then everybody started laughing. I still don't know to this day what in the hell was so damn funny.

As we prepared for our twenty-five-mile, full-backpack speed-march, the drill sergeant came back around to tell me that I had best cover my neck. He told me that if one of the commanding officers were to see my love bites, there would more than likely be hell to pay. But I was not about to cover anything up—I could not have been more proud of than Jackie Dee's love bites, especially when I remembered how she had affectionately applied each one. I thought, what's the worst thing these instructors could do to me—use harsh language while kicking the shit out of me? I didn't think they could do anything worse than what I had already suffered back on the block.

By that point in my life I'd been in multiple car crashes, been hit with a baseball bat, a car jack, bricks, and pop bottles, and been sliced with knives, just to name a few things. I really didn't mind a little physical pain every now and again, anyway. I always thought that it helped to stimulate my senses, and it was instrumental in keeping me sharp, alert, and on my toes. However, what I could not seem to tolerate was emotional pain, especially where Jackie Dee was concerned.

Due to some mandatory weekend military training exercises, it was several weeks before I would get to see Jackie Dee again. I also got into fisticuffs at a local drinking establishment with this drill sergeant from another platoon who had too much mouth and not enough brains, that resulted in my losing a couple of my weekend passes.

9

The Dream of a Lifetime

A week before Easter of 1978, Jackie and I made plans to meet in Waynesville, a little town just outside of Ft. Leonard Wood, Missouri. Jackie would catch the bus in Sedalia, which would bring her into Waynesville. I called ahead to reserve a room for us at a motel.

The day we were to meet, I arrived in Waynesville about a half hour earlier than she did and waited for her outside of a diner next to our motel. It felt like it had been such a long time since we had last been together; in reality, it had been about a month. It devastated me to be away from Jackie even for a single day, let alone a few weeks. I stood outside the diner, smoking a cigarette and waiting for Jackie's bus to arrive, and I finally saw it approaching. The bus came in on time, and as she was getting off, I watched her looking around for me.

Just then, Jackie caught my stare. To my utter shock and amazement, when I saw those persuasive eyes, coupled with that seductive smile; my heart skipped a beat, and then it felt like it just dropped into my stomach. I couldn't get over how lovely she looked—I literally just gasped. As Jackie began to walk toward me, I just stood there frozen, unable to move a muscle, admiring how strikingly beautiful she was. What a remarkable sight to behold she was; that moment has left its impression in my heart and mind for life. I will never forget the way she looked just then.

Jackie Dee was wearing a scarf around her neck, a light, mauve-colored blouse, and these tight-fitting jeans that revealed just how attractive and shapely her figure was. It still makes me quiver just to think about it. Moreover, the best part of all was that Jackie was here to spend the night with me. Let me tell you something; for me personally, it didn't get any better than that. I didn't waste another second trying to figure out how I had gotten so lucky before I took Jackie into my arms and held her ever so close to me, never wanting to let her go.

Jackie was supposed to take the bus from Sedalia to Kansas City for the Easter weekend, which we both had planned to do in the morning. But first, this was our night to holler.

We had supper at the diner before retiring to our room, where I had drinks waiting for us. I can remember holding Jackie in my arms that night so vividly; she looked and smelled the way angels ought to look and smell. I was completely swept away by her beauty, her charm, and her body's seductive fragrance.

With the exception of the first time we had ever made love, this night was by far the most passionate evening we had spent together to date. That night you couldn't have separated the two of us with dynamite because we were so into each other's love all … night … long. Jackie's and my love was blossoming into what could only be defined as a "ferocious love."

In the morning, Jackie and I had breakfast at the diner, and then we both took the bus back to Kansas City. When we arrived, we boarded a local bus that took us within a couple of blocks of where we lived. I walked Jackie to the corner of 24th and Chelsea and held her in my arms as I kissed her good-bye. We still could not take the chance that anyone might see us together for fear of the problems they could cause us once again. After all, her parents and our neighbors had no idea that we had been seeing each other all along for those past few months.

Jackie and I got together as much as we possibly could over that Easter weekend. My mom had two cars now, and I was able to use one of them, so Jackie Dee and I could go just about wherever we wanted.

That Saturday afternoon, I borrowed Mom's car to go to the cemetery where my dad was buried. But I had been drinking that morning, and as I was driving through the little town where he was laid to rest, I was pulled over by the police and arrested for driving under the influence—again. Fortunately, they let me sleep for a couple of hours in a jail cell there and then released me on my own cognizance with a signature bond.

On the night of Easter Sunday, Jackie and I planned to ride the bus out of Kansas City together. The bus would drop Jackie off at Cole Camp Junction, which was about fourteen miles west of Stover. Jackie's grandmother Maxine would pick her up there, and I would continue on to Ft. Leonard Wood.

Jackie's parents dropped her off at the bus station; I had already arrived fifteen minutes earlier so that I wouldn't be spotted by them. In fact, I had already boarded the bus and was sitting in the back, waiting for Jackie Dee. She got on the bus and sat next to me, and boy, things got god-awful hot in the back of that bus. We held each other almost the entire hundred-mile trip into Cole Camp Junction.

I wonder if Jackie Dee remembers that night. It is a wonder that I can still remember that bus ride, but I remember it just like it took place this morning. It's amazing to me that I can remember things Jackie and I did together more than twenty-five years ago in such detail, often more accurately than I can remember things that happened last week.

Not long after that Easter weekend, I finished my training, and I processed out of Ft. Leonard Wood on my twentieth birthday: April 17, 1978. Once I finished processing out of Ft. Leonard Wood, I headed for Stover, Missouri, where Jackie was finishing the school year. In a nutshell, I was now a twenty-year-old man—sexually involved with a fourteen-year-old girl, in a much-heated love affair that was hotter than a six-alarm fire in a bamboo-and-canvas hut.

We stayed in Stover until the end of the school year, and then we said our good-byes to grandma Maxine and headed for Kansas City. When we got back there, we tried to live our lives more openly and saw each other whenever we wanted.

I took the first job I could get, which was as a merchandise sorter and dockworker for Sears and Roebucks in North Kansas City, until I could find something better. It was difficult for me to find work in the various fields in which I had trained in the Army; Kansas City used unionized labor in the areas that had caught my interest.

Well, no sooner had Jackie and I tried to live our lives and continue to develop our relationship openly—her parents tried to interfere again and keep us from seeing each other. Jackie's fifteenth birthday was just a month away, and we knew that in the state of Missouri, we could get married soon with at least one parent's consent. This is exactly what the two of us wanted. Jackie continually told her parents, "Look, either you allow me to see Daniel, or I'm taking off and moving in with him." But Jackie's parents did everything they could to prevent her from seeing me, which usually meant trying to ground her, taking away her phone privileges, and so forth.

When Jackie had finally had enough of their prying and meddling, she told them, "I'm out of here," packed her belongings, and left with me. Jackie and I moved in with my brother and his wife in the northeast area of Kansas City. After we had been living there for a couple of weeks, my mother called me at work to tell me that Jackie's mom had been trying to get hold of Jackie. She asked me to relay a message to Jackie to call her mother as soon as possible, and that was all she said.

On Tuesday, July 18, two days before Jackie's fifteenth birthday, we walked up to the Stop and Go convenience store at the corner and used the pay phone to call her mom. In that phone conversation, Jackie's mom told her, "Fine, if you want him, then you can have him, but I'm not going to sit up night after night worrying about you, young lady. You do whatever you have to do to set this thing up, and then you call me, and I will meet you downtown at the courthouse to sign the papers allowing you to marry him." Before her mom hung up the phone, she said, "I hope you're happy, Jackie."

When Jackie got off the phone, she looked at me with that same smile I had seen so many years ago that had forever captured my heart. She said, "Guess what? My mom is going to sign the papers so that we can get married!"

When I heard this, I thought I was going to have a coronary right there on the spot. I thought, "My God in heaven, can this be true, or am I dreaming? Is this really happening?"

I do not think you could have found another couple anywhere on the planet who were happier and more excited than Jackie and I were on that most memorable day. It felt like a great weight had been lifted off our shoulders, and now we could take a deep breath and relax. Or could we?

Jackie and I were hugging and kissing each other and jumping up and down out in front of the store as if we had just won a million dollars. I'm sure passersby's must have thought that we were drunk or stoned out of our minds from the way we were carrying on, but if ever there was a time to celebrate, this was it!

Even though I was now living with the girl of my dreams and I knew that we were soon to be married, I was still plagued by reoccurring nightmares of how I had lost Jackie back when my dad had just passed away. I just could not seem to shake them off, but when I drank alcohol, it seemed to help me sleep better at night. It was just like when I was at Ft. Leonard Wood; some of the guys whose bunks were near mine used to wake me up when I moaned and cried in my sleep because of these haunting dreams.

Anyway, on Jackie Dee's fifteenth birthday that Thursday, we went to my family doctor for the blood test that was required by law in those days. I still have our blood test results to this day. Then we called her mom to tell her that we had taken the blood test and that we needed a little more time to prepare a nice wedding. Jackie's mom refused to give us more time and insisted that we get married as soon as possible—within the next week or two, if not sooner. This really angered and bothered me; I wanted Jackie Dee and me to have a nice, memorable wedding so that we could have something really special to look back on. Nevertheless, given the circumstances, Jackie and I conceded the point—her mom having even taken that decision away from us.

Jackie and I came to the conclusion that her mom was probably trying a little psychological exercise; she may have wanted to see if I would actually go through with marrying Jackie Dee if I had to do it immediately. This was an utterly ridiculous notion, of course, when getting married was exactly what Jackie and I had been wishing, hoping, and praying for—for almost a year. Then again, her mom also might have thought that if we did go through with the marriage, it probably wouldn't last very long.

I was able to find a minister who was willing to conduct our marriage ceremony on such short notice. The minister's name was Reverend E. Paul Fisher, and the marriage ceremony was scheduled to take place at the Kensington Baptist Church, located on the corner of 24th and Kensington in Kansas City, Missouri. We set the date for the evening of Saturday, August 5. That did not give us very much time to prepare, so we really had to scramble to get everything ready.

On Friday, August 4, 1978, the day before we were to get married, we met Jackie's mom downtown at the Jackson County Courthouse. Jackie's mother was true to her word, and she signed the necessary documents, giving her consent for Jackie Dee and me to marry. Thank you, God!

Jackie's mom tried to lecture us about what we were getting ourselves into at every opportunity, but Jackie and I did not hear a word she was saying. In fact, it sounded like she was speaking some kind of foreign language or something. Jackie and I had fought so long and so hard for this that we just wanted to be left alone together. We were two young lovers, emotionally involved and devoted to one another so strongly that we would surmount any obstacles that stood in the way of our being together.

As you can imagine, the anticipation, the anxiety, and the excitement that we both felt leading up to the wedding ceremony was nothing like anything either one of us had ever experienced before. This was to be our day, our wedding day.

We met at the church, where we could feel the tension building between our families. When I saw my bride, Jackie Dee, in her wedding dress for the first time, something suddenly seemed very familiar about it. Then it dawned on me what it was. In that moment, in my mind's eye, I was transported back to that day so long ago when I'd stood across the street from Jackie Dee and seen her smile for the very first time. This was what I had seen in my mind's eye on that day; it was her and me together on our wedding day, standing side by side, her clothed in her wedding dress and me in a tuxedo. And now, it was all being fulfilled like a dream come true. As the reality of this engulfed me, coupled with how lovely Jackie Dee looked in her wedding dress, I simply could not stop my heart from racing or my head from spinning.

Up until this point in time, there had been four times in my life that I'd literally had to hold on to something to brace myself upon seeing Jackie Dee. The first was when I was absolutely captivated the first time I ever saw Jackie Dee's smile. The second time was that day I saw Jackie at the swimming pool, wearing her two-piece, white bathing suit—yikes! The third time was when Jackie and I were standing on my front porch and I could see a glow around her, not to mention that her seductive body fragrance had had an ambrosial, intoxicating effect on me that had left me breathless and dizzy that day. And the fourth was when she got off the bus in Waynesville, Missouri and I saw those persuasive eyes and that seductive smile; and this would be the fifth, seeing Jackie in her wedding dress for the first time. She looked absolutely stunning.

I just could not get over the fact that this was really happening; now she was going to be all mine, my beautiful and precious wife. I thought, "What have I done to deserve Jackie Dee's hand in marriage, this beautiful girl who has had such a stronghold on my heart since she was a little girl and who still wows me every time she walks into a room?" I had watched Jackie Dee grow up in stair-step fashion over the years, and now she was utterly breathtaking. The answer, of course, was that I hadn't done anything; she had fallen in love with me. But I still hadn't ever told Jackie about my dreams or that she was in fact the girl of my dreams.

During the wedding ceremony, I held Jackie Dee's hand in mine as the Reverend asked us to state our wedding vows. Jackie became so nervous that I thought she was going to pass out. I could feel her knees starting to buckle just a bit, so I moved in closer to her to help hold her up and keep her from losing her balance.

On Saturday, August 5, 1978, around seven-thirty in the evening, Jackie and I were united in holy matrimony. That night, we promised each other before God and man to love and cherish one another in sickness and in health, for richer or for poorer, for better or for worse, and to forsake all others and cleave to one another as long as we both would live. The Reverend, sanctioned by divine authority, pronounced Jackie Dee and me husband and wife in the name of the Father, the Son, and the Holy Spirit. Then he said, "What, therefore, God hath joined together, let not man put asunder." Then the Reverend turned to me and said, "You may kiss the bride."

As I held my bride to kiss her, I looked into her eyes and I thought, "With all that I've done wrong in my life—I must have done something right to be blessed with Jackie Dee's hand in marriage." Jackie and I then kissed each other for the very first time as man and wife and breathed a sigh of relief. We had finally won a long, hard-fought battle to be together, and now—much to our delight—the wedding ceremony had finally taken place.

The ceremony and the circumstances leading up to the ceremony had put Jackie and me under so much stress that we really couldn't enjoy it like we would have been able to do under more pleasant circumstances. But in the end, we had just what we wanted, and that was to be husband and wife. It was official, Jackie Dee was all mine, just as much as I was all hers.

For me, this was a dream come true—literally. I mean it was truly a miracle that I could be so fortunate to have such a beautiful bride as this heavenly creature standing there before me as Jackie Dee was on that day. From that day forth, for as long as I would have a breath of life in me, I gladly gave Jackie Dee all of my tomorrows.

Thank you, God, for giving Jackie Dee to me and making that the greatest day of my entire life. It will forever be the greatest day of my life.

As we were leaving the church, I thanked the Lord for hearing my prayers and bringing her back to me. We left with our marriage certificate in hand.

Jackie's family had arranged to have a little wedding reception for us at her sister's, so we went over there. I must say that what Jackie's family had prepared for Jackie Dee and me on such a short notice was all very nice. I still have every picture that was taken of us together during our wedding reception.

After the reception, we headed back to my brother's place, where we were staying until we could find a place of our own. I carried Jackie Dee in my arms out of the car, up the stairs, across the sidewalk, up three more flights of stairs to the door, and then inside. We collapsed onto the sofa with Jackie Dee on my lap, still in her wedding dress, and we just looked at each other in utter disbelief. We just could not believe that we were now husband and wife.

But I wasn't going to waste another second trying to figure out how I'd gotten so lucky—to finally be holding the most beautiful girl in the world, the girl of my dreams, but now as my wife, Mrs. Jackie Dee Gutridge. And we lived happily ever after ...

Well, not quite. There were still some heartaches and heart-breaks on the horizon, but it sounded nice to write that anyway.

We had not been living with my brother for very long before Jackie's mother found us a house for rent on Lister Street, which was just one block over from Chelsea Street. It was a cute little two-bedroom house with hardwood floors, and the property owner lived next door. Jackie and I were both a little suspicious about the whole matter, so we proceeded with caution, and we moved into the house on Lister.

While we were living with my brother, Jackie had worked at Send-a-Card and in the radiology department at Osteopath Hospital, both of which were within a couple of blocks of where we lived. Unfortunately, Jackie had to quit both jobs when we moved into our new home on Lister Street because it was too far away. I had to pull reserve duty once a month for the U.S. Army, and I was still working at Sears. I transferred to the main Sears complex, which was within walking distance of our new home, so things were really coming together very nicely for us.

In those days, I was working all the time, sometimes double shifts, but sometimes I took some time off work to spend time getting close and intimate with my wife—Jackie Dee. Sometimes it seemed like we stayed shut up in that bedroom for days, only coming out to take restroom and refreshment breaks. Then it was back to our bedroom and into each other's arms, neither of us ever wanting to let go. It was so precious and sweet, the way we would just cling to one another. I will remember those days forever.

Jackie and I had the most wonderful time getting lost in each other's love; we truly found paradise within the blankets, sheets, and pillows that lay on our bed. Jackie Dee truly made lovemaking memorable and something very special indeed. Later on, we would make homemade pizzas, drink tall glasses of chocolate milk, and sit out on the back porch making each other laugh and just acting silly.

One of the hardest things I ever had to do was to leave Jackie to go to work each morning. She would stand there at the door with this precious, seductive smile—and scantily dressed, I might add—that on occasion I just could not leave her. I would end up calling in sick just so that I could spend the day with her.

I learned very quickly that Jackie was very meticulous about keeping the house spotless, and everything had to be very organized. Jackie was a very neat and tidy person, so I started to become that way as well. In fact, I still am to this very day.

That year, Jackie and I went to Lake Jacoma for a Labor Day picnic with some relatives from my side of the family. I think my family really liked Jackie because she always carried herself so well, she was such a likeable person, and she was so cute. We had a very nice time, the weather was perfect, and it was a beautiful day. We wore ourselves out playing everything from football, to softball, and catch with a Frisbee. Later in the day, we thought about going for a swim in the lake, but we were extremely exhausted by then. We got a lot of sun that day and were both pretty well cooked. When we made it back to our home that evening we could hardly cuddle up to each other because we both were so sunburned, but we found a way.

When the first semester of school was about to begin, Jackie's mom tried pressuring her into returning to high school. However, because of the social tension and civil unrest that existed in those days in our neighborhood and especially in the area high schools, we thought it best for Jackie to apply for her general equivalency diploma instead.

Her mom then began trying to persuade Jackie to start attending church with her again. One Wednesday night, Jackie and her mother went to church. I was upset about this because it was the same church at which she had met Mark, her ex-boyfriend. When it came time for Jackie to return home from church that night, I planned to act like I hadn't waited up for her and had already gone to bed. So when I saw them pull up in front of the house, I jumped off the couch and sprinted for the bedroom. However, I slipped on a throw rug and slid across the hardwood floor, through the dining room and all the way into the kitchen. I somehow ended up under the kitchen table, entangled with the kitchen chairs.

I heard Jackie come through the front door, and I tried not to move a muscle at first because I didn't know if I had hurt myself or not. Then embarrassment began to settle in. I didn't want her to see me under the table like that. Well, she didn't see me at first, but then she looked around for me and found me under the table. She asked me what in the world I was doing under there. I told Jackie what had happened with the rug and told her that I really didn't want her to go to that church anymore after what had happened the last time she started going there. I told her that it just brought back a lot of bad memories for me.

Jackie said, "If it means that much to you, then I will never go back to that church again." To her credit, she stayed true to her word, and she never went back there again.

We stayed at the farm in Stover for a few weeks of September and into October, with the exception of the two weekends that I had to pull my Army reserve duty. Jackie and I were helping her grandparents build a new house. We cut and nailed down every floor joist and wall stud in the entire house. Later, we also cut and nailed down every piece of redwood on the exterior of the house. We also stayed there to take care of the farm so that her grandparents could take care of some business back in Kansas City. We had the whole place to ourselves, and we had some great times together with no one around to bother us for miles. We reminisced about my weekend visits to the farm just a year and a half earlier and about some of the shenanigans we used to pull in the wee hours of the night. Only now, we could come and go as we liked and do whatever we wanted to do.

When we were away from everything and everybody and I had Jackie Dee all to myself, like I did during this time we spent at the farm, that's when I was most confident about her love for me. Any time we were by ourselves, I could feel her love all around me. On the other hand, when she was around her family or her friends, she would act different and was not as close or affectionate with me, though I was never really sure why.

10

It Was the Best of Times, It Was the Worst of Times

While we were at the farm, Jackie and I took breaks from working on the house every now and again so that we could spend some time getting close and intimate with one another, as newlyweds will do. We were content and happy just enjoying each other's company all day long, and then came the nights. We were truly inseparable. In retrospect, we had always enjoyed each other's company very much and gotten along very well, even when we were kids. Jackie and I shared many interests other than each other's company and love, among which were movies, horses, swimming, and especially music.

While we were away from the house on Lister, the sewer backed up and flooded the basement. The landlord wanted us to pay for the damages and the plumbing bill even though we were away at the farm in Stover when the incident occurred. While we were still at the farm, Jackie's mom and grandparents arranged to have all our stuff moved out of the house on Lister. They moved all of our possessions into the house that Jackie's grandfather Harry lived in, which was coincidentally located back on Chelsea Street.

Jackie and I lived with her grandfather Harry for about six months when we returned from the farm, which kept her family very much involved in our relationship and caused us some problems from time to time. Harry asked us to help take care of the house on Chelsea and to continue working on the house at the farm on occasion, so we did what we could to help out. I was still working at Sears and pulling my weekend reserve duties once a month, and Jackie worked in various jobs and kept the house up.

On occasion, we went up to Penny's house for a few drinks, and Jackie began to notice that if I had too much to drink, my behavior would become somewhat unpredictable. Sometimes I would be kissing Jackie and hang all over her, and sometimes I was prone to fits of anger about things that happened early on in our relationship. God knows I tried to keep any of that stuff from surfacing, but sometimes it would just come out when I was under the influence of alcohol.

Well, it did not take long for Jackie to tell me that she simply did not want me to drink around her any more, so I stopped drinking in front of her. The problem was that I had developed such a strong dependency on alcohol that I could not just walk away from it cold turkey like that. I was not an everyday drinker, but sometimes I really needed alcohol to help me cope with my issues of self-worth and to deal with the fact that I was never really accepted into Jackie's family, even after we were married. I wanted to believe that I did have some worth and that what I had to say did matter; and that if I spoke one word aloud, then that thought would live on long after I was dead and buried. But I just could not shake those demons of doubting my self-worth that had plagued me in the past, especially during the time that I was trying not to drink around Jackie. I began to hate everything about myself all over again, and I couldn't seem to get rid of those god-awful nightmares that I often had.

One of the other things that kept troubling me in those days was the fact that Jackie's ex-boyfriend Mark was still going over to her mom's house, supposedly to fix things. The son of a bitch would often just so happen to show up at her mother's place when Jackie was there visiting, and I would always somehow conveniently be at work. These visits were brought to my attention by our nosy, gossiping neighbors, who always thought it was their moral obligation to report everything anyone ever said or did. This would always spark a chain reaction of memories in me—I would remember the time she broke up with me for that prick-shit around the time my father had passed away, or the time she'd lost her virginity to that shit-hole, or seeing those hickeys on the back of Jackie's neck the year before, and so forth.

In addition to these issues, I was having some problems with my first sergeant in the reserves, mostly concerning the length of my hair. I was also having problems at my other job over my work-schedule, and the fact that we were still tied to Jackie's family had me scratching my head for some kind of solution or relief. Furthermore, I was still being haunted by those same reoccurring dreams that literally made me moan and cry in my sleep. The nightmares were not just about losing Jackie Dee back in '76, although this experience did dominate most of my hellish dreams. Some of the dreams were about the things I had suffered in Catholic school or at other times in my youth. On top of everything else, I was still being tortured by memories and nightmares about losing my young friend Johnny, an experience for which I could never forgive myself.

I tried smoking grass again, but as I mentioned already this had an adverse effect on me—it elevated my heart rate and made me irritable, cranky, and apt to become violent. Then the after-effects of it would make me want to hang all over Jackie like some kind of love potion was working on me, and believe me, I didn't need any help in that area whatsoever. I just wanted to be with the girl of my dreams without any strings attached, but I wasn't strong enough to pull it off, and I found myself given in to her all the time.

One day, my friend John called me on the telephone and said he needed my help with a problem he was having with some people in his apartment complex. Apparently, some guys in his apartment building had made some inappropriate comments and gestures toward his wife, and he wanted to confront them about it. I told John I would be right over.

Now, Jackie did not like my friend John, and rightly so—if I was ever in any kind of trouble, he always seemed to be involved. I knew that my going to help him might start an argument between Jackie and me, so I did not tell her where I was going. Instead, I made up some excuse to leave the house, which turned out to be a big mistake on my part. But I needed to blow off some steam really badly, and so I thought that this was just what I needed. Besides, I knew deep down inside that John would have some adult beverages there waiting for me.

Sure enough, he did. After John and I threw down a couple of cold beers, I said to him, "Let's go bust some heads."

We went upstairs and knocked on the door of the apartment where the guys who had made the comments lived. A woman answered the door, and we asked her where the man of the house was. She said, "He ain't here. He's where he always is this time of night—at the bar on the corner."

We said, "Okay, thanks—we'll check it out."

John and I went back to John's apartment to get the birthday present I'd bought for him that year—a policeman's night-stick—and I brought my lefts and rights. We drove up to the bar on the corner and jumped out of the car as if we were racing to put out a three-alarm fire. We ran up to the front entrance of the bar, I kicked open the door, and we went inside. John swung his club and nailed this guy in the head who happened to be sitting on the barstool closest to the front entrance. It made such an awful thud that it scared the shit out of everyone seated or standing in the place. They all started screaming, and they sounded like a bunch of woman.

I yelled out, "That's right, you bastards—it's payback time! Who's next?"

Then I turned and swung my fist, bashing this guy in the jaw as he tried to run out the front door. My punch knocked him over a table and into the jukebox, and it started playing "*Love Me Tender*" by Elvis Presley.

There probably weren't more than six or seven people in the bar that night, and we nailed them all to ensure that we got everyone who'd been involved in making remarks about John's wife. That is excluding the bartender, since he dove out the window and ran away.

As we were making our exit, I grabbed a beer off of the bar. I drank it down as we headed out the door to the car and finished it by the time we got there. From across the street, I swung the empty bottle in a hook-like fashion over my head.

It sailed over the top of the car—across the street, right toward the bar's huge, front window, which was all lit up with neon lights that flashed on and off. The bottle hit dead center, setting off what look like a fireworks display in front of the bar and out onto the sidewalk and street.

Yes, it was payback time for what those guys had said to John's wife, and we got a couple of innocent bystanders in the process. It felt like old times again, drinking and fighting—this was the sort of nightlife my friends and I had been involved in when Jackie had left me for that shit-ass back in '76. If John and I could not find anybody who wanted to fight us, then we would go to the cemetery and fight each other until we were both bloody messes.

Anyway, to keep from being arrested that night, John and I hid out from the cops in the cemetery. One of the guys we assaulted identified John to the cops—after all, he lived in the same apartment building—but they only had an eyewitness description of me. We went to my dad's grave and drank there all night. Eventually, John was arrested for what we had done, but he never snitched on me.

I knew there would be hell to pay when I returned home to Jackie Dee, and she really let me have it good. She accused me of being with another girl, which was a joke. Then she threw a stereo receiver that my dad had bought for me just before he died, and it struck me in the head.

I did not go into all the details of what I had done the night before, but I assured Jackie that at no time was I in the company of any female, nor did I ever have any desire to do so. Jackie told me that if I ever pulled a stunt like that again, she would pack her stuff and move back home. But she continued to insist that I not drink around her, and I really needed a drink at least once and a while—or so I thought.

Our second Christmas together came and went, as we helped usher in 1979. We continued to live with Jackie's grandfather

Harry through April, which was also when I turned twenty-one years old.

Jackie and I had often talked about having a baby to help stabilize our marriage, but she couldn't become pregnant no matter what we tried, so we consulted an obstetrician. After the doctor examined Jackie, he said that it would be very difficult for her to become pregnant. Her uterus was tilted in such a way that it may even be impossible. In addition, if she were to become pregnant, this would more than likely cause some problems for Jackie and the baby. Therefore, he advised against us even trying.

Before we were married, Jackie and I had talked about having a baby as a way to coerce her parents into letting us get married. But now that we were married, we wanted to have a baby to start a family of our own. Needless to say, the doctor's analysis hurt the two of us very deeply.

Back at the homestead, Jackie and her grandfather Harry started arguing over everything from what to make for dinner to what to watch on television. One day when Jackie and her grandfather got into a pretty good argument (I'm not sure what it was about), Jackie said, "That's it, we're moving."

It just so happened that Jackie's great-grandmother Elsie was getting to the point at which she could no longer take care of herself properly, since she was around eighty years old. So we moved in with Elsie, who also lived on Chelsea Street. Now we were living right across the street from Jackie's parents, which did not help matters between Jackie and me one bit. We also found out very quickly that we had to keep an eye on Elsie or she would leave the gas for the stove turned on without lighting the burners.

July and August came and went, and we celebrated Jackie Dee's sixteenth birthday and our first wedding anniversary. It was around this time that we purchased our first car from a man named Ripley, believe it or not, who lived on the corner of 23rd and Quincy, three blocks over from Chelsea. The car was a 1973 Mercury Comet with a black vinyl top and a red body. It had a little 302 V-8 engine that had lots of power.

I remember teaching Jackie how to drive it; she was so eager to learn, and I was just as excited about teaching her. We had a great time with our little driving lessons. Jackie picked it up very quickly, and I was so proud of her. She wanted to drive all the time, all over the city and its outskirts. We would stop at 7-Eleven and get a tall Slurpee, then drive around smoking cigarettes; talking about the things we enjoyed doing together, and listening to love songs on the radio. Jackie and I would get lost on purpose to see if we could find our way back home, and the two of us just had a blast. We could easily drive more than a hundred miles in a day just cruising around town together.

It wasn't long before my friend John called me up again and said that he needed to talk to me because he and his wife had gotten into a huge fight. John wanted my advice on what he should do. In reality, I think John really just wanted someone to drink with him so that he could forget about everything for a little while. John said he would meet me later that night at Penny's house, where Jackie and I had first gotten back together.

I felt obligated to go through with meeting John because he had covered for me a number of times when I was in a tough spot. Besides, my addiction for alcohol was stronger than Jackie's ultimatum. As bad as this sounds, my drinking was the only thing that seemed to be able to help me stand myself. The alcohol also helped me to cope with my suspicions about what was really going on between her and Mark, since he was still coming around her mother's place. I believed that Jackie's mother was either trying to play matchmaker between him and Jackie or attempting to break us up in some other way. One time I accidentally came upon a letter that Jackie's mother had written her that validated those suspicions.

Overall, I just did not feel good about myself. It didn't help matters that I had to keep my hair short for the military reserves. After all, this was still the seventies, for goodness sake. And as if I didn't already have enough things troubling me from my past and present, I always felt that Jackie was one hundred times more beautiful than I could ever be handsome. I had often dreamed and imagined that in another time and place, Jackie Dee would have been a princess in a kingdom some-where, and I would have been only one of the many suitors try-ing to seek an audience with her for only a fleeting moment.

I think it is very important to mention that for all the time I had known Jackie Dee, she was anything but conceited about her looks. I'd never observed Jackie flaunting her personal endowments even once during the whole time I'd known her. She was extremely modest about everything.

On this particular day that John telephoned me, I desperately needed a drink of alcohol. So after Jackie fell asleep, I slipped out the front door and met up with him and Jackie's friend Penny. We pulled an all-nighter and consumed so much whis-key—mainly Jack Daniel's Black Label—that I couldn't tell my left hand from my right. I was so drunk that I could not even remember what my name was.

When the sun started coming up over the horizon, we were all sitting in the front seat of our car. With the one good eye that I could still see out of, I saw what looked like Jackie walking down 24th Street toward us. I thought for a second that I was hallucinating, but I wasn't. It was Jackie Dee Gutridge, my wife, and she had come up there looking for me. How Jackie knew I was there is still a mystery to me to this very day. Penny had her arm around me—she had been trying to come on to me, but with no results. I was in such bad shape that I was like one of those store-bought mannequins; you had to position me upright in the seat just right, or I would fall over.

When Penny saw Jackie approaching, she quickly withdrew her arm, and all I could do was moan in disapproval that her arm had been around my shoulder at all. I was so out of it that I couldn't even open the car door to get out. When I finally did get that damn car door open, I fell out onto the ground and passed out.

John started giving Jackie a hard time about her wanting to take me home, and began pushing her around a bit. I was so out of it that I couldn't lift a finger to help her. I had to wait for another day to pay John back for putting his hands on her. And I paid him back good one night when he least expected it with a hard right to his jaw, and then I made him apologize to her. Jackie Dee loaded me back into our car and drove me home, where she practically had to carry me inside and put me to bed.

Later that day, after I had sobered up a little, Jackie remained very calm about the whole matter, and she was actually so nice to me that I wondered what she was really up to. After that incident, Jackie didn't even mind if I started drinking around her again, though that was a mistake. I could never seem to keep my mouth shut about things that had happened between us in the past or about what appeared to be happening right under my very nose. It was around that time that Jackie also started to drink a little more alcohol than she had before.

I was now working two jobs—one at Good Year Tire Company as a mold man and one part-time for Sears—and I was still doing the monthly army reserves bit. Jackie worked days at a place called Filtronetics, which made computer chips. She also worked nights at Dunkin' Donuts out on 23rd Street in Independence. Before Jackie went to work, she would dress so smartly and do her hair and makeup so attractively that she would get outrageous tips from guys who were also always asking her out.

One night, Jackie was coming to pick me up at work, and as she slowed down to stop at the corner of our block, a man tried to force his way into the car. Fortunately, Jackie had the car doors locked, but the man began trying to smash through the driver's side window with a flashlight. Jackie hit the gas pedal, floored it, and sped away around the corner. She was so scared and upset when she finally arrived at my work that I could hardly calm her down long enough for her to explain to me what had just happened. When she told me that someone had been trying to get her, I told Jackie, "I'm going to kill me somebody—slide over."

I drove as fast as I could to our street, and when we got there, we saw several police squad cars. We found out that a man fitting the same description had just stolen Jackie's grandfather Harry's truck. Harry's truck was stolen from just up the street from where this thief had tried to force his way into Jackie's car. As the thief was making his getaway in the truck, driving recklessly down the street, Harry jumped into the back and tried to break out the back cab window. Later that night, a few miles away, the thief lost control of the truck and crashed, killing

Harry. Eyewitnesses at the scene said they spotted two men limping away from the scene of the accident. To this day, they have never been caught.

I felt really bad that Jackie had to suffer through the pain of losing a loved one—it just crushed me to see her suffer so. That night, we made the drive down to Stover, Missouri to break the news to Jackie's grandmother Maxine. When she heard the tragic news, Maxine fell to her knees and just cried and cried. We gathered around Maxine right there on the floor and wrapped our arms around her to comfort her and cry with her.

The next morning, we all returned to Kansas City to lay Jackie's grandfather Harry to rest. Grandma Maxine never returned to live at the farm again; instead, she moved in with her mother, Elsie, Jackie's great-grandmother. Jackie and I moved back into Harry's house on Chelsea, where we'd been living just six months earlier. We had some great times together in that house, and now that Jackie was drinking a little more, I think she was a bit more relaxed.

However, one day I came home from work and found a Dear John letter, which Jackie had left for me on our dresser. It said that she was leaving me and moving back in with her mother, but it really didn't say much more than that.

I immediately drove over to her mother's house and walked up to the front door, which happened to be open. I went on in, and Jackie's mother appeared.

She asked me, "What are you doing here?"

I said, "What do you think I'm doing here? I've come to take my wife back home with me."

She started in by making her usual idle threats, and so I let her have her fun; after all, I was standing in her front living room. Jackie must have heard our voices from upstairs, and she started to come down. I looked at her, smiled, and said in a soft, calm voice, "Babe, are you ready to go?"

I swear, that's all I said to Jackie, and she said, "Yes, I am."

I helped Jackie get all her things together, and as we were carrying all of it out the front door, her mom started in on her. Jackie didn't stop to argue or even look back. She just turned to me and said, "Let's get the hell out of here."

When we got into the car, I did not ask Jackie anything about why she had left me. I thought that if she wanted to talk about it, she would when she was ready. As I lit a cigarette for her and one for myself, she began telling me about how her mom had called her early that morning, after I had left for work. Jackie said that they had talked for hours over the telephone, and before she knew it, she was packing up her things and heading for her mother's house. She said that she was sorry about the whole thing, that it was all a big mistake, and that she would never do anything like it again. She went on to say that there was no way in hell she would ever move back in with her mother and step-dad again.

One time while I was pulling guard duty for the army reserves, I found a little puppy that someone had dropped off by the side of the road. I picked the puppy up and brought it home to Jackie. She just fell in love with it, and she named our puppy Sissy.

We stayed in Harry's old house on Chelsea Street until around Jackie's seventeenth birthday in 1980, when we purchased a new trailer home. We had it set up at the Heart of America Trailer Court. The trailer was so big that it took up two lots. It was a brand new trailer home with a nice bay window in the kitchen. It had central air, three bedrooms, two bathrooms, and a utility room with a washer and dryer, and it was carpeted throughout. It was fourteen feet wide by seventy-five feet long, and it was very nice living space for us.

The experiences we had while living in our new home during the next year were both some of the most intimate and memorable and some of the most painful of our marriage. We had gotten away from the watchful eyes of just about all Jackie's relatives—I say "just about" because her sister lived right across the street from us at the trailer court. Nevertheless, I felt like I had Jackie Dee all to myself, for the most part. We had so many precious moments together in our new home that it felt like things couldn't get any better. Or could they?

The summer of 1980 was a very hot one. Jackie and I sunbathed just outside our back door all summer long with tall drinks in hand. We kept an electric fan blowing on us to help us stay cool, as we relaxed in our nice lounge chairs. In the afternoons, we headed back into the comfort of the central air and wore ourselves out loving each other from one end of the trailer to the other while listening to rock and roll. In the evenings, Jackie and I sometimes went to rock concerts or to local drive-ins and then went for long moonlight drives. Then we headed for home, where we cuddled up together and got lost in each other's love all … night … long.

It was like what heaven ought to be like with the girl of my dreams—Jackie Dee.

11

The Dream Receives Its Final, Fatal Blow

Jackie and I drank adult beverages together now, and I was doing a good job of keeping anything that might cause us to quarrel from surfacing. Things seemed to be going very nicely when one day Jackie returned home from her mother's—or at least that's where she said she had been—and I noticed that she wasn't wearing her wedding ring.

I asked her, "Babe, where's your wedding ring?"

I know it surprised Jackie; she hadn't been home five minutes before I noticed that the ring wasn't on her finger. But you see, I always looked for the ring that I had placed on her finger the day we were married. I liked to show Jackie Dee off in public because she was so attractive; she was an absolute knockout with her captivating smile, and she had such a shapely figure that she could turn any man's head. I was so proud to call her mine, and that wedding ring was a symbol that she belonged to me, but now she wasn't wearing it.

Jackie could not give me a straight answer at first, but she finally came out with it. She said that her ex-boyfriend Mark had it. When I heard this, I tried without success to slow my heart rate down and to pull myself together. I'm sure you can imagine the state of mind I was in. With tears in my eyes, I asked Jackie, "How the hell did that shit-hole get our wedding ring off of your finger? And what in God's name were you doing with him that he could get close enough to you to take it from you? Just tell me how it happened!"

I never did get a straight answer from Jackie about how he'd gotten the ring in the first place, but she did tell me that he'd put our wedding ring in his mouth and was chewing on it when she last saw him.

I cannot describe to you the heartsick feeling that came over me from head to toe in what felt like wave upon wave of shear frustration and disappointment. I'm telling you, you couldn't have wounded me any more deeply or pierced my heart with greater precision and accuracy than I was standing there crushed in my living room on that day, even if you had planned it. I was fighting back tears, and I could not think of anything to say to Jackie besides, "Let me have a moment, let me take a minute for myself." Then I closed my eyes in an effort to compose myself. I was in such a rage that I could not even see straight. In that moment, I could feel a pounding—throbbing sensation beginning to develop inside my head. Everything before my eyes was a total blur. I told Jackie that I needed to get some air and that I was going for a drive.

She must have read my mind because she knew exactly what I was going to do. I was going to get our wedding ring back and kill that motherfucker who had been a thorn in my side for far too long already. Jackie literally hung on me and begged me not to leave. She told me over and over that her mom would get the ring back from him.

Throughout our relationship, these kinds of things made me doubt whether Jackie really loved me. They obviously caused me to be suspicious of her. Moreover, they forced me to keep my heartfelt emotions in check. In fact, they kept me from being able to share with Jackie any of the true feelings that I had for her in my heart. For reasons I've already mentioned, I had pretty much kept my emotions at a superficial level up to this point in our marriage in order to keep from getting hurt. At least try to minimize the damage that was being inflicted upon my heart from time to time.

I stayed there with Jackie until she fell asleep that night. Then I gathered up a 30.06 rifle with some 220-grain bullets, a revolver, a hunting knife, a hacksaw, hammer and nails, some rope, some duct tape, and a pair of gloves.

I know it sounds like overkill, but I always believed in being prepared for whatever happened.

I'm not exactly sure what I was going to use the hammer and nails for, but I remember thinking over and over that I was going to nail his ass. Not only was I going to recover the ring, but I was also going to make that shit-hole die a slow—tortuous death, and to hell with the consequences.

I stopped at a local convenience store and bought a couple pints of Jack Daniel's. I began drinking it down as I drove over to Mark's house. When I pulled up in front of the house, I saw a light on inside, and so with the revolver in my hand and hidden under my left arm, I walked up to his front door and knocked. An old woman answered the door, so I asked her if Mark was home. She said, "What do you want him for?"

I said, "He has something that belongs to me, and I want it back!"

She said, "He's not in right now, but I expect him back tonight, I just don't know exactly when."

I said, "Okay, I'll come back later."

I got back in the car, drove around the block, and parked a few houses up the street so that I would be able to see him when he pulled up. I sat there in my car, nursing my bottle of whiskey with tears in my eyes and wondering what was really going on around me and if I was really being played for a fool. All the things that were going through my mind really pulled me down, like being so full of doubt about my self-worth. Coupled with the thought of how my one and only dream, Jackie Dee, was slipping away right through my very fingers, even though I felt like I was doing everything possible to hold onto her.

As I sat there, I could feel my heart breaking apart inside of me. To make matters worse, the inside of my head was still pounding from earlier that day, but now had intensified. Just then, a myriad of other bad thoughts from the past also began to bombard my heart and mind. Then, all of a sudden, I saw a figure who looked like Jackie's ex-boyfriend Mark walking up the front sidewalk.

I quickly got out of my car, closing the door very quietly behind me, and approached the figure as I came out of the darkness. I walked right up to him undetected, and without hesitation, I stuck the gun right in his face. Just then, I noticed that it was not Mark but someone else—shit! I startled him as he stood there shaking just looking at me waiting to see what I was going to do next. He began begging me not to shoot him—then threw his hands above his head, and with the gun still pointed at his face; he lowered his right hand as if to reach for something, when just then I smacked him hard across the face with the gun. He staggered backwards holding his face, then threw his wallet at my feet and ran away. As I kicked his wallet out into the street, I suddenly realized that he must have thought this was a hold-up.

Through it all, I never uttered a sound. I just walked back to my car, got back in, and waited. As I sat there in the car, I wondered what Jackie would think if she happened to wake up and I was not lying there in bed beside her.

Anyway, I sat there all night long, nursing the pints of whiskey until they were all gone—in between taking restroom breaks behind some trees in a nearby, vacant lot. Then daylight came, and there was still no sign of Mark. I must have dozed off, and I woke up when I heard a tapping on the driver's side window. It was a Kansas City Police officer. I rolled down the window and asked, "What seems to be the problem, officer?"

The officer said, "One of the neighbors spotted you parked out here for quite some time and thought they had better call it in." Then he asked me what business I had being there.

I told the officer that I had been drinking at a friend's house the night before and that as I was driving home, I began to feel really sick. I had decided to pull over and rest for a little bit, and I must have fallen asleep until I heard him knocking on my window. He asked me if I felt well enough to drive home, and I told him I thought I could manage well enough. He asked me where I lived, and I told him I lived at the Heart of America Trailer Court.

He said, "Well, that's not far at all, you'd better move along." I told the officer to have a nice day, and then I drove away.

I could not believe my luck. The officer had not even asked me for any identification or searched the vehicle. On my left side, the loaded rifle was sitting between the seat and the door. Had he opened the driver's side door, the rifle would have been in plain view. The handgun was sitting under my legs in the front seat. I had everything else on the floorboard behind my seat in an overnight bag. I was very disappointed that I had not gotten to finish what I'd set out to do, but I was very much relieved that I had not been thrown in jail. I thought about going back home to Jackie, but I decided to go straight to work instead.

When I got off work that day, I was still very upset over the missing wedding ring. I went over to my mother's house to cool off and to drop off the guns as well as the other items. I slept there on the sofa for a couple of hours. When I woke up, everyone was gone, so I headed back home to Jackie. Before I could even get in the front door, she started asking me where I had been and accusing me of one thing or another. I was still extremely upset over the wedding ring incident, but I thought that if I could not say something to Jackie in a calm and pleasant manner, I had best not say anything at all. I especially didn't want to talk about anything that was really on my mind or tell her where I had been or what I had been up to.

Jackie started apologizing about the ring again and assured me that she would get it back. I told her that I did not want her going around that shit-hole. She said she had talked to her mom and that she was getting the ring back from him.

I set out again to recover our wedding ring myself the very next day. This time I just took the revolver with me. I decided to walk right up and shoot him in the face like I almost had done back in '76.

Mark's car was not parked out in front of where he lived, so I drove around looking for places where he might possibly hang out. In the late hours of that night, I was pulled over and arrested for driving while intoxicated. In addition, I was charged with operating a motor vehicle without a valid driver's license, since mine had been suspended for quite some time now. The car was impounded at the police tow lot. Fortunately, they never searched the vehicle and found the gun that I had hidden under the front seat or even the bullets in the glove box.

I could not get hold of anyone to get me out of jail besides Jackie, but I really didn't want her to know that I had even been arrested. I thought I could have my mom bail me out and keep Jackie from ever finding out, but I could not reach my mom or anyone else. When Jackie came to bail me out, she let me have it good, accusing me of everything under the sun. Then she started in about my drinking problem and told me that she wanted me to stop drinking alcohol entirely from that day forth, or else.

However, I could not stop drinking alcohol. I had become completely dependent on it as a means of escaping, being able to stand myself, and coping with what was going on between Jackie and me. I was in the middle of a power struggle between trying to hold onto the girl of my dreams and battling my dependency for alcohol, and I was losing both.

I never did hear all the ins and outs of how Jackie got our wedding ring back from that shit-ass, but I guess her mom had something to do with it. Either that or Jackie just simply bought another one.

Not long after that, my friend Pat came to visit me from out of town. You may remember him as the guy whose car I torched that one night at the drive-in. We caught up on old times while driving around town all day long drinking whiskey. Soon we were both pretty inebriated. Then, as if we weren't already fractured out of our minds, Pat broke out some weed and wanted me to smoke it with him. I refused at first, but I eventually found myself giving in to his continual bickering and whining. We smoked one joint after another as we continued driving around drinking whiskey.

I could feel the effects of the alcohol but not the marijuana, or so I thought.

Just then, I thought I saw Jackie's ex-boyfriend Mark approaching a four-way stop intersection that we were also approaching. I stepped on the accelerator and floored it, speeding toward the intersection. My friend Pat began yelling at me to stop the car, but to no avail. Instead, I sped up and ran through the four-way stop sign, broad siding the other vehicle. We plowed into the car with such force that the vehicle spun around several times and ended up on the sidewalk. My friend Pat was knocked unconscious, and he ended up on the floorboard of my car with a collapsed lung. I escaped without so much as a scratch.

I jumped out of my car, ran over to the vehicle I had just crashed into, and started punching the driver in the head. The car door wouldn't open, but I was in such a rage that I got him into a headlock and tried to pull him through the window. I could not pry him from the vehicle because his body from the waist down was pinned between the seat and the steering wheel. Just then, I noticed that this guy was not Jackie's ex-boyfriend toad-faced—shit!

These guys from a nearby forklift repair shop heard the crash and then witnessed me punching and choking the driver. They ran over, got hold of me, and wrestled me to the ground. They held me until the police arrived. I was arrested for a litany of charges, and a couple more years were tacked onto the suspension of my license. I had to apply for a hardship license just so that I could drive back and forth to work. I remember sitting in jail and thinking about how that asshole, that is my wife's ex-boyfriend had to be the luckiest guy in the world to be able to take the girl of my dreams' virginity and now our wedding ring. To make matters worse, I keep missing the damn Mark—shit!

Fortunately, the man I had crashed into was not seriously injured. I never saw my friend Pat again. Whenever I was in serious trouble, such as during this incident I would retain one of the best lawyers in the state that money could buy. I spent a lot of money on lawyer's fees, restitution fees, and court costs trying to get out of all that mess. I had our car totally restored and we had it back on the road again in no time.

Needless to say, things were a bit rocky between Jackie and me from that point on. There were just too many questions and doubts going through my heart and mind for me to ever be at peace. After all this time, I was still being haunted in my dreams concerning the first time Jackie had left me, and now I was afraid of losing her again. What was her ex-boyfriend really doing at her mother's house all the time? Not to mention, the hickeys on the back of Jackie's neck the day of the concert, and now the wedding ring incident. All of these things kept swirling around in my mind and haunting my dreams, and sometimes the terrible things that had happened to me in my youth would also rear their ugly heads and torture me.

It was now the summer of 1981; Jackie had just turned eighteen, and I was now twenty-three years old. It was around that time that Jackie started to have her night out with the girls and go to dance clubs. I didn't mind it at first, but then there started being occasions when she didn't come home at night. We argued about this a lot, so I started going to the dance clubs with Jackie even though she really did not want me to go.

At these dance clubs, it seemed like some guy was trying to put his hands on Jackie every time I turned around. Even the guys in the band made advances at her. I mean, I literally had to beat the guys off of Jackie, which I didn't mind doing, but I eventually had to get her out of there because there were just too damn many of them. Either that or I was going to call some of my friends for backup. However, Jackie had become so hooked on the attention she got from all the guys, the heavy drinking, the nightclub setting, the dancing, the music, and all of it that there was no way in hell she was going to give it up. Moreover, it was becoming an everyday ordeal. It appeared that Jackie was developing her own fan club of guys and girls who liked to watch her dance and hang out with her.

We argued over this issue more than we had argued about anything else in our marriage.

Finally, one day Jackie started dropping that word that no man who sincerely loves his wife ever wants to hear—divorce.

It became clear that I would have to take the chance of losing Jackie again or let her do what she wanted, which meant letting her go to these dance clubs without me. Rather than take that chance, I found myself giving in and letting Jackie do whatever she wanted. It was not long after that day that Jackie stopped coming home at night again; and sometimes she wouldn't even come home the next day.

One day while I was trying to talk to Jackie about her not coming home at night, the bottom completely fell out and she told me she was leaving me. The reason Jackie gave me was that she needed to get away to have some time to think things over. Now, any guy who's ever heard that line knows that what it really means is, "I'm not done using you by a long country mile." A woman who says that just wants to rake your heart over the coals and inflict enough pain that you think you are going to die. By that time, there is no life left in you anyway and you might as well be dead.

As Jackie was packing her stuff in the trailer, I became so enraged that I started punching walls, windows, and everything else but her. I was acting like a real jerk and making a spectacle of myself, but I just could not believe what was happening. I had always felt that Jackie Dee was too good for me to begin with and that it would be a tall order to keep someone like her, who had so much to offer, satisfied with a bum like me. Of course, it had been a tremendous struggle to make her mine in the first place. I knew full well that it wouldn't take long before Jackie started seeing somebody else, but even so, I wanted to keep holding onto my dream.

As I watched Jackie leave that day, my heart began to break all over again, just like it had before. I watched from the front living room window as she drove away, and I wondered what was going to become of my dreams and me now that it was over. I had just lost paradise for the second time; there went the girl of my dreams, out the door and down the street. I vowed not to sleep in the bed in which we had shared so many precious moments until she returned. Jackie never did return, and the bed was never slept in by either one of us again.

The love I had to offer Jackie simply could not compete with the new nightlife, attention, and companionship she had found, and my drinking problem had not helped things either. Jackie Dee was too young, too beautiful, and too powerful for my love to be able to hold her in my arms any longer. She had it all working for her.

Jackie moved in with her grandmother on Chelsea Street, where she was able to enjoy her freedom and come and go as she pleased. She was now an eighteen-year-old knockout on the loose.

She was finally getting to enjoy her freedom and sow some wild oats, which she had never been able to do, having married me so young.

During the next few months, I tried to hang around Jackie Dee wherever I could find her; for a few measly crumbs of attention that she pitifully threw my way here and there. I chased after Jackie like some kind of lost puppy looking for its owner. I gave up the trailer, moved back in with my mom, stepped up my drinking, and took drugs at an overdose pace. I even took a job as a cashier at a gas station where Jackie worked at the time just so I could see her on occasion. All the while, I was still working at Sears, Montgomery Ward's, and doing the reserve bit for the army.

Two months later, I was fired from the gas station job for pulling a gun on someone who was trying to rob the place with a knife. I confronted the robber, stuck the gun in his face, and yelled at him to drop the knife or I would shoot him in the face. When he dropped the knife, I wrestled him to the ground. I held him face down with his arms folded behind him and my knee on the back of his neck until the police arrived. According to management, I was supposed to let him rob the place and take whatever he wanted, but I just could not resist the temptation to take out some of my aggression on that shit-head. No charges were ever filed against me for carrying the hand-gun, thank God.

One time, I was successful in tracking Jackie down at one of the dance clubs. She was always so hard to find; it seemed like she had always just left each place I went. This time, I caught up with her at a club she frequented. We had a few drinks and danced together, and I asked Jackie where things stood between us and if she still loved me. Jackie said she just didn't see how things could ever work out between us considering this new lifestyle she was now living. She said that she still loved me but that she wasn't in love with me. Now, any guy who has ever heard this line knows that it really means, "I'm divorcing you as soon as possible, but to avoid a scene with you right here and now, I want you to believe that I still love you."

One of the rare times that Jackie actually took one of my calls during this time, she told me that she was in the process of filing for a divorce and that her parents were paying for the divorce proceedings. Hearing this drove me into a deeper and darker depression than I had ever thought possible, and I just could not recover. I found it very difficult to even get off the couch. I had always been so full of energy, and I was never a lazy person by any stretch of the imagination, but I just could not shake off this dark cloud hanging over me.

While Jackie and I were apart, I suffered from chest pains and headaches so severe that even alcohol and drugs had little to no effect on them. The more time that elapsed without my seeing Jackie, the worse the chest pains and headaches became. On the other hand, when I did occasionally get to talk to Jackie over the telephone or see her, the pain would somewhat subside temporarily. This caused me to believe that the pain I was experiencing was directly tied to Jackie Dee. I was convinced that if I had her back in my life, I would be cured of all that was ailing me.

On one particular day, the pain in my chest and head was so severe that I thought if it were possible for a man to die of a broken heart, I would be dead by morning. I just did not want to go on living if I could not have Jackie Dee in my life. I was not sleeping at night. The pressure in my chest and head was so intense that I sometimes blacked out even when I was not under the influence of any stimulants or depressants.

Finally, I went to see my doctor. He ran me through all kinds of tests and asked the usual line of questions. The doctor's diagnosis was that the pain in my chest was due to a tremendous amount of stress and lack of sleep. He went on to say that I needed to change my lifestyle or that I would probably be dead in a matter of weeks. To sum things up, I was suffering from clinical depression. He prescribed me some anti-depressants along with something to help me sleep at night. The last thing he told me was that a change of scenery wouldn't hurt either.

None of the medications helped ease the pains in my chest or the throbbing headaches, and I was still not able to sleep at night. The pain, coupled with my heavy drinking and smoking, made me into a walking zombie.

On the rare occasions that I was fortunate enough to be around Jackie Dee, I had to put on a big front and pretend that everything was okay. Jackie simply did not want to hear about it, when actually I was shriveling up and dying inside. Putting up this façade for Jackie and hiding the pain that was killing me was one of the hardest things that I ever had to do.

Sometimes the pain would get so severe that I felt like an elephant was sitting on my chest and like I was being crushed and suffocated. Then I would vomit profusely and black out. Why was this all happening to me? Why wasn't I able to let her go and get on with my life? Why wasn't my heart and mind able to get out from under this spell I was under?

I could not understand where this pressure in my heart and in my head was coming from, nor could I understand this powerful force that would never allow me to let Jackie Dee go. At no fault of my own did I do anything to bring this on. I did not ask for this—it just happened. My heart never had a chance from that first day I saw Jackie Dee smile. Just like that, I was her prisoner of love forever.

The pain in my heart and head would never subside long enough for me to catch my breath or think clearly. Jackie was still holding all the keys to my heart, just like the first time she left me. The pain had been simply unbearable back then, and now it was literally killing me. The difference was that this time, all the alcohol I consumed was not helping me, and neither were the medicines the doctor had prescribed for me.

We spent Thanksgiving and Christmas apart, although I did get to see Jackie briefly on Christmas Day. Jackie and I spent New Year's Eve together with some friends, and we all went bowling. I got a chance to hold Jackie Dee in my arms and kiss her for the last time when it came time to ring in the New Year of 1982, and believe me, I made it count. I felt so much better that night just being in her company; I could not take my eyes off of her, but I knew it wasn't going to last.

Whenever Jackie saw me or talked to me on the telephone, she never missed an opportunity to remind me that she was divorcing me. At the same time, she kept me hanging on a string so that she could continue to use the car and borrow money from me from time to time. Even though I knew I was being used, I didn't care. At least I got to see her, hear the sound of her voice, and maybe—just maybe—even steal a kiss from her, if I was lucky.

I found out through a mutual friend of ours that the girl of my dreams was now involved with someone else. Jackie didn't have any qualms about owning up to this, throwing in the reminder that she was divorcing me anyway.

I was now at rock bottom; the only way that I could sink down any lower was the grave itself, which was looking pretty good to me right then. The only thing that kept me hanging on was the chance that Jackie might call me to borrow some money or the car. Now, how pathetic is that? But it was something over which I had no control. It clearly had taken on a life of its own, and I had no say in it whatsoever.

Eventually, I had to quit hanging around Jackie altogether to keep from getting hurt even further, if such a thing were even possible. I just couldn't stand hearing from those precious lips of hers that she didn't love me anymore, that she couldn't stand the sight of me, and that she was divorcing me.

12

One Foot in the Grave

Jackie's and my relationship was now reduced to—don't-call-me, I'll-call-you basis.

Throughout the years of my so-called love life, I had often wondered: if love was a teacher, then why was it so hard to learn? I knew if I were to have any kind of a chance at winning back Jackie Dee's love that it would take a miracle. I would also have to do something about my drinking as well as the other vices that plagued me. The drinking was such a big part of my life by that point that it dominated almost every other aspect.

You know, not all stories have a happy-ending, and this was shaping up to be an unhappy ending—for me, anyway. I started remembering the game I used to play with my revolver, but rather than fiddle around with it, I thought long and hard about just ending it all right then and there. By that point in time, the pain that was suffocating me from within and the pressure that was constantly pounding inside my head had become so great that I just couldn't take another day of it, not even another hour. Therefore, I decided it was time to bow out of Jackie's life—and this life altogether—but first, I had to see the girl of my dreams just one more time.

I cannot believe after all these years just how great the pain was over losing Jackie Dee and making the decision that would ultimately cause me never to see her smile again. The smile that had captured my heart so long ago that even now as I write this portion of this story, I cannot keep from crying.

You know something? If I could look into the faces of all the women who have ever walked the face of the earth since the beginning of time, I'm convinced that I would never be able to find anyone with that beautiful and mesmerizing smile like that of Jackie Dee Gutridge. The pain I felt is still there after all these years, and I am afraid it has wounded and scarred me so deeply that I will feel it for the rest of my life.

Anyway, I just had to see Jackie Dee one more time, and I decided not to tell her that I was going to take my own life. There are two sorts of people who consider suicide. One type of person tells someone about his plans with the hope that they will try and stop him from doing something he doesn't really want to do. At this point, he is reaching out for help. The second sort of person decides to commit suicide, tells no one, and gets on with it. His days of reaching out for help have long since ended. I didn't tell anyone anything. I strongly believed that this was the only way to cure my twice-broken heart and put an end to all my pain and suffering.

On Friday, March 19, 1982, I set out to look for the girl of my dreams, hoping to see her smile one more time before I took my own life. I stopped and purchased some whiskey, then drove around to all the places where Jackie usually went, but I could not find her anywhere. I have never shared this with anyone until now, but I had decided that if I could not find Jackie that night, I would head to the cemetery where my dad was buried and take my life there at his graveside.

I went from one place to another, threatening people everywhere and accusing them of lying to me concerning her whereabouts, when I was again pulled over by the Kansas City Police and arrested. Needless to say, I did not pass go, I did not collect two hundreds dollars—it was back to jail for me. This time, the police took me straight to the county lock-up to sleep it off until someone could come and get me out the next day.

I tried to sleep late that night and into early the next morning, but I couldn't rest for the pain that was throbbing in my chest and head. It had me tossing and turning in those uncomfortable racks that they called beds. As I lay there, I thought about what a miserable failure I had become.

I couldn't keep the girl of my dreams happy and content by my side, and I couldn't even take my own life without screwing that up either, at least for now anyway.

A few hours later, early in the morning, the county guards brought us some black coffee and some cinnamon rolls hard enough that you could smash and kill the cockroaches with them. Then they let all the inmates wander out into the courtyard to smoke cigarettes, but all I could think about was Jackie Dee and taking my own life to get rid of this heart-wrenching pain.

As I looked around, I could see that there was an eight-foot fence surrounding the compound with double prongs and three strands of barbed wire at the top.

I went back inside and lay in my rack, and I started to think about the sum total of my life. I suddenly realized that I had hardly been out of the state of Missouri. In my heart and mind, my greatest accomplishment was marrying Jackie Dee and now she was gone, which obviously meant everything in the world to me. Sometimes the truth isn't always a pleasant thing; and in my case, the truth was that if I could have made a pact with the devil to get Jackie Dee back into my life, I would have done just that. For the brief time she was mine, I truly believed in my heart and mind that she was worth living for, worth dying for, and worth going to hell for.

When I closed my eyes, I could see Jackie Dee back on that day when I'd stood there across the street from her and seen her smile that gave me my first and only romantic dream more than ten years earlier. In my mind's eye, I could see the first time we kissed and the first time we came together. Just then, another dreamlike sequence started to overlap this first one.

In this dreamlike sequence, I could see myself running to the fence around the compound. I could see myself scaling the side of the fence, and then I saw myself hanging by the throat from a set of the prongs atop the fence. I saw my throat gashed wide open and my blood squirting out in all different directions, running down the front of me and the fence and dissipating in the dirt below. I now knew how I could end it all right there where I was being incarcerated at, and so I made up my mind that this was how I was going to do it. I thought, "Hell, I'll die laughing if I can just do this one goddamn thing right."

I wanted to see Jackie one last time, but I simply could not stand the pain in my heart and my head for another second. I thought, after I'm dead and shoveled into my grave, will Jackie Dee ever know just how much I really did love her? Probably not, because I could never tell her for one reason or another, mostly because of my suspicions about what was really going on around me. Moreover, I thought that if I did share everything that was in my heart with her, it would make me vulnerable or expose me in some freakish way. So I kept my heartfelt emotions hidden, and now it was all too late.

Through all of this, from my first heartbreak through to being on the verge of taking my own life, I never once directed any anger at Jackie Dee in thought or in deed; my heart simply would not allow it. In my heart and mind, Jackie could do no wrong. I placed the blame for losing paradise twice entirely on myself, and now I was ready to pay the price for losing her with my life.

Just then, one of the guards announced that we all needed to line up to make our phone calls to someone who could pick us up. I'd decided that I wasn't going anywhere but the county morgue. That was going to be my next stop. But then I thought if I couldn't see Jackie one last time, I could at least hear the sound of her voice, before getting on with this last thing I felt I had to do, that would end all my heartache and suffering.

I quickly got into line to make my phone call. The pressure in my heart and head was so great that I had to fight for control to keep from passing out as I waited for my turn to make a call. As I was waiting, I started to shake uncontrollably; I knew that it was partially from the pain I was in and partially because I needed a drink of alcohol so desperately.

Finally, my turn came, and I tried to get hold of Jackie Dee, but as fate would have it, the line was busy. I tried calling over and over for the five minutes I was allotted, but to no avail.

I told myself, doesn't that figure? It was the girl of my dreams that I was trying to call for the very last time, and now the dream was over. I could have gone to the back of the line and tried all over again. However, I decided to just get on with what I had already decided to do. I would work my way out into the compound to smoke a cigarette, and then I would hang myself on the fence. By the time anyone could get to me, it would all be over in less than a minute. As I walked back to my bunk, with tears in my eyes I asked God to forgive me for the way I had turned out in life and for what I was about to do. I had stuffed my cigarettes up under my mattress, and I decided to have one last smoke before ending it all.

Just then, I felt something force me to my knees right there beside my bunk, and I could hear myself crying out, "Please, God, make a way when there seems to be no way to bring Jackie back into my life! If there is a God in heaven, help me, or I'm going to kill myself."

Now, I was not a religious man by any stretch of the imagination, nor was I the lapdog of Satan either, but between the two, I was most certainly closer to being a child of the devil than I was to being a child of God. There were very few times in my life when I had offered up a plea to God Almighty. In fact, the only time I had ever offered up any kind of request in the form of a prayer was when it concerned the girl of my dreams—Jackie Dee. If this was what it would take to get her back into my life, then so be it. Nevertheless, after I had cried out those words, "Please, God, make a way when there seems to be no way to bring Jackie back into my life! If there is a God in heaven, help me, or I'm going to kill myself." The thoughts of suicide came rushing back into my mind.

But as I rose to my feet to get on with it, something drove me back down onto my knees again. Then something began to penetrate my heart, and it felt similar to what I had experienced back on that first day that I saw Jackie Dee's smile. However, this was even greater and even more enthralling—I could feel God's love pouring down over me.

In the twinkling of an eye, the pain that had been in my heart and my head was completely gone. All the filth, darkness, and violence that were so much a part of my life and all the things I was in bondage to; the drugs and alcohol was being flushed right out of me. Somehow, I understood in my heart what was happening to me. I knew in that moment, crumpled on my knees, that this was without a doubt—the hand of God sweeping over me in answer to my prayer I had just offered up to Him. In place of all the darkness and addiction that had filled me, I was infused with an inner strength like nothing I had ever experienced before. This inner strength gave me confidence that was unparalleled by anything I'd ever felt before.

All of a sudden, I was very confident about where my life was headed, as this profound awareness began to sweep over my heart and mind that I would never smoke, drink, take any drugs, or punch anyone in the face that didn't absolutely deserve it ever again. But the greatest and most miraculous part of all of this was another awareness that began to settle into my heart and my mind. I suddenly knew beyond a shadow of a doubt that Jackie Dee would return to me and that we would start the family that we had always wanted to have together.

When I received the last part of this revelation, I jumped to my feet. I got so excited over all that was happening inside me that I thought I was going to break out into some kind of cele-bratory song and dance. I thought, I had better get a handle on myself or they will think I've gone mad. And for a split second, I began to wonder about that myself, because everything was suddenly different. I mean, everything about me was different, including my thought process. Everything I could see, touch, taste, and smell now seemed different to me in a good and wholesome way.

The drug and alcohol addictions that were once embedded in my heart and mind from the time I would wake up in the morning to when I would pass-out at night were completely gone. Even my desire for cigarettes, which having smoked since the second grade was completely gone. For the first time in a long time, I felt absolutely no cravings or even the slightest urges for any of those things.

It was all gone in a split second and replaced by—the only way to explain or describe it is it was if I was being infused with this light and this light was forcing all the darkness right out of me. Obviously, light and darkness cannot occupy the same space; much like when you turn the light on in a darkened room, the darkness has to flee. Well, that is exactly what had happened to me.

I wondered why a miracle of such magnitude had been bestowed upon someone as unworthy as I was. To be the recipient of all these attributes that I was being infused with in place of all my vices. Then it dawned on me that I must have touched God with my plea, in that he had heard my heart's cry, and God in turn had mercy and compassion on me.

Feeling very much beside myself, I made my way into the latrine, trying desperately to maintain some kind of control because I was so giddy. It suddenly seemed like I was walking on air, and when I looked in the mirror, I could see that I had this big smile that seemed to be stuck on my face. For the life of me, I wanted to tell someone, anyone, what was happening inside of me, but who? I thought that anyone I tried to tell would probably look at me like I was crazy or something. I tried to calm myself down the best I could, but I just simply could not. The emotions that were bubbling up inside of me were so overwhelming that I simply could not contain them. So I started to tell the guards and the other inmates what was happening to me, all the while displaying this big, uncontrollable smile on my face.

I began to wonder how in the world I could explain to someone else what was happening to me in a way that they could understand, even though I myself understood the source and origin of this miracle. I simply could not put into words nor was there anything within the realm of knowledge or logic that could help me to be able to explain this miracle that was taken place in my heart, mind and body. I could explain it no better than the soldiers who were guarding Christ's tomb after the crucifixion could explain how the stone had been rolled away. Only now, the stone had been rolled away from my heart so that Christ himself could enter in. How can anyone explain a miracle? You just can't—it is what it is. All I could say to those around me was, "I wish I could open myself up so you could look and see what is happening inside me." This day, this wonderful, miraculous day, Saturday, March 20, 1982, was the first day of the rest of my life.

Just then, a guard came around and said, "This is the last reminder: if you have someone to call who can come and pick you up, you'd better do it now, or you'll be here until Monday."

I called my brother and asked him to come and pick me up. He said that he and his coworker would be there in about an hour. When my brother and his friend arrived to pick me up, I started telling them what had happened to me. Then I backed off a little bit and just told them about the various things I would never do again, like taking drugs or drink alcohol and so forth. They just nodded their heads and said, "Sure, sure you won't."

I asked them to please stop over at the house where Jackie was now living before they took me home, so they did. I'm telling you, the sky had never looked so blue, and the grass had never looked so green, and everything was more beautiful to me than ever before; even my sense of smell was keener and sharper. I told my brother that they could drop me off there at Jackie's house and that I would walk home from there.

I walked up to the front door of the house, so full of excitement about this new lease on life—having been given a second chance, and the joy that kept bubbling up inside of me caused me to display this big smile on my face. I felt like I had just come back from the dead, and that I could see and appreciate everything more clearly now than ever before.

I knocked on the door, and Jackie answered it. She seemed somewhat disturbed that I was there, and she asked me, "What are you doing here?"

As soon as I saw Jackie, I thought, "What a sight for sore eyes—she looks even more beautiful than ever before! Wow!" I responded, "Honey, you're not going to believe it, but something wonderful has happened to me."

Tears welled up in my eyes as I told her, "If I could just open myself up so you could take a look inside of me, you would see that I am a changed person through and through."

Jackie responded by reminding me that she was divorcing me and that I shouldn't have come over there. I told her that I understood that but that I'd just wanted to stop by and share with her that something wonderful and miraculous had happened to me. I told her that I couldn't explain it but that it was a miracle. I said, "I have changed—you just wait, you'll see."

Jackie told me that I had better leave, then asked me if she could borrow some money and have the car later that night. I said, "Sure, that's fine, just give me a call later over at my mother's." I told her that I loved her so very much and that I looked forward to talking to her later about what was happening to me. I headed for the door and started to walk home when

I noticed that my brother and his friend were still waiting out in front for me.

Apparently, my brother had thought he'd better wait for me, because he said I was acting very peculiar.

13

The Resurrection of a Dream

You know, even though Jackie had reminded me about the divorce and I could see that the changes in me had not changed her in any way, none of that could overshadow the inner strength, confidence, and joy that seemed to be guiding my every step. And along with all these attributes with which I had been blessed, I had also been blessed with patience. Thank you, God.

Once I was back at my mother's, I had an ever-increasing desire to learn more about the God who had given me back my life. I began telling my mom and anyone else who would listen what had happened and what was continuing to happen to me. My mom just looked at me as if I had flipped my lid or something. I asked my mother if there was a Bible in the house, and she gave me my dad's Bible, which had belonged to his mother. It was a King James Christian Bible. I started thumbing through the Bible and reading bits and pieces, but that did me no good, so I started reading it from the beginning.

Jackie called me later that day to tell me that she had changed her mind about borrowing the car and the money. She said that she needed to stop depending on me for things since she was divorcing me.

I said, "Whatever you say, honey. I'll be here for you if you need me."

Jackie asked me, "Are you okay?"

I said, "Yes, I've never felt better." I tried again to explain to her what had happened to me, but she said she had to go. I told Jackie that I loved her very much and that I missed being with her immensely.

When I finished talking with her, I delved back into the Bible for an hour or so. Then Jackie called me back again and said she had changed her mind again about borrowing the car. So I delivered the car, some cash, and a kiss to Jackie Dee that night and tried to explain to her again about what had happened to me. However, we couldn't talk for very long because she was running late to where she was headed that night.

Even though I was still so very deeply in love with the girl of my dreams, my passion and desire for her was now ever so slightly overshadowed by my desire to learn more about the God who would inevitably bring Jackie back into my loving arms. That night, I read the book of Genesis, making my way through fifty chapters in one sitting. During the next three weeks, I devoted myself to prayer and fasting. By the end of the third week, I had read the entire Bible and had fasted for all three weeks—drinking only tea. I broke the fast on the twenty-second day, April 10, a week before my twenty-fourth birthday.

What I surmised from reading the Bible cover to cover was that this was God's love letter to us and that God truly walked on every page. This was our standard, our plumb line through this life and the life to come. As far as I knew, it was the only book ever written with instructions on how you could live forever. In addition, if you applied these biblical principals to your life, you could find the answers to your problems as well as success. Lastly, it revealed how to harness the power of God and make your dreams and the desires of your heart come true.

One morning, I was doing some cross-referencing on some scriptures when I heard a knock at the door. It was two young men from a local church in the area. They were going door-to-door, handing out invitations for a social gathering with free victuals and bowling at a recreation facility. My eyes fell on the scriptures that were on the invitation; they were the same scriptures I had just been cross-referencing that morning. We did not talk for very long, but I told the two young men that if I could make it, I would see them there.

One of the passages was Hebrews 11:6, which reads, "But without faith, it is impossible to please God, for he that comes to God, must believe that he is God, and that he is a rewarder of them that diligently seek him." For me, this would be the most important scripture in the Bible. This passage was the key to unlocking so many other important scriptures. In addition, this passage explained that faith—that is, trusting and believing in God and his written word—is the key to finding favor with God. In turn, he will supply you with your daily sustenance and give you the desires of your heart.

Faith was the key, but where could one find this faith? Could it be purchased or found somewhere on or in the earth? I found the answer in Romans 10:17, which read, "Faith cometh by hearing, and hearing by the word of God." When you wholeheartedly endeavor to reach out to God through his written word or in any other capacity, it shows that you have the faith necessary for God to hear your heart's cry, supply whatever is lacking, and give you the desires of your heart.

I went to the social gathering at the bowling alley, and to my surprise, I was accepted and made to feel welcome by everyone. There were many people there who had similar backgrounds and were recovering from drugs, alcohol, and just about everything else that there was to recover from. I shared my story with them, and it wasn't long before I started getting invited to men's breakfasts, prayer meetings, and churches. Every time I turned around, I was being invited to share my testimony at one social function or another; it seemed like I was in demand all the time.

Jackie, as it turned out, heard about my conversion from everyone but me. Each time she called me at my mother's; I was either at work, or at church, or at prayer meetings and Bible studies. On Easter Sunday, I was able to persuade Jackie to attend an Easter service with me at a local house of worship. We went out for breakfast afterwards, and we really had a nice time together. Jackie looked absolutely gorgeous in the burgundy-colored dress she wore that day; it warranted taking more pictures of her. We really did not get a chance to talk things over that day, though, because I felt that the timing just wasn't right, so I waited.

In the three-week period following my conversion, I walked around the streets sharing my new, profound, life-changing experience with anyone who would listen to me. I talked to my family, my friends, and even strangers about the God that walks on every page of the Bible. I learned very quickly that the people who had known me before were all very suspicious of me, and rightly so. I was so out of control before, but now instead of carrying a gun, I was carrying a Bible.

The word spread pretty quickly around the neighborhood, and everyone wanted to know what had happened to me. I resisted talking too much about it to my family and friends because I felt that the best approach was to let them see the change in me—kind of a walk-the-talk mentality.

On Friday, April 16, 1982, the day before my twenty-fourth birthday, I took a leap of faith and booked a room at a motel for the weekend. I was hoping that I would be able persuade Jackie to come and stay with me away from everything and everybody so we could talk things over. Believe it or not, Jackie said yes, she would come and stay with me; she probably agreed because she remembered it was my birthday.

While Jackie and I were at the motel, she was all over me, and she wanted to know what was causing me to act so differently. She wanted to know what was really going on with me, since she had been hearing so much about it from everybody. Jackie could sense that something was obviously different about me—my demeanor, the way I looked, the way I talked, everything about me, really. And for the first time, I was finally able to explain to Jackie everything that had happened to me the morning of March 20. However, I did not tell her what my motivation had been behind the prayer I had offered up to God that morning; in fact, I didn't tell her until just recently, almost twenty-five years later. I couldn't tell her at the time—in that moment my mind was solely fixed on figuring out a way to get her back into my life; when—just like that, the miracle that would forever change my life had occurred, saving me from myself on that miraculous morning.

Instead, I told Jackie that I had cried out to God that morning by saying, "If there is a God in Heaven, help me, or I'm going to kill myself." And then, in that moment—the life changing miracle occurred. I was fearful that if I did tell Jackie what my motivation had been behind my prayer that she might have thought that it was all a ploy to stop her from divorcing me, and to ultimately convince her to come back to me.

I also did not tell Jackie just then what had been revealed to me about her coming back and starting a family with me. Instead, I waited. I wanted her to come back to me of her own free will, not because she'd heard me ramble on about this or that. In my heart and mind, I just knew that it simply wouldn't work any other way.

That weekend at the motel, Jackie and I had the most wonderful time together. It was as if we were falling in love all over again, though I had never fallen out of love with her. We went for drives to get tacos or pizza, then headed back to the room, had our meal, and went for a swim. At night, we went for drives and walks on the Plaza, then went to see movies. We took some pictures of one another at the motel that I still have to this day. The two of us really had a nice time enjoying each other's company, and it seemed just like old times again, only minus the alcohol, drugs, and cigarettes.

During our stay at the motel, Jackie and I were also able to get many things out in the open. Although Jackie told me that she was not ready to give up the nightlife that was so much a part of her life now, I told her, "That's okay, honey; I'll be here for you if you need me." That whole weekend, Jackie just kept saying, "You're different,—there is something unusually comforting about you. You seem so relaxed; it's like there's this mysterious calm and peacefulness about you."

Jackie was right; instead of the strained look that I always used to wear on my face, I now carried around a big smile that caused my face to ache by the end of the day. Sometimes my ribs would ache from laughing and giggling about my transformation from near-death experience to being so full of life and about the promises that were still to come. I was a very happy person indeed, thanks be to God. There was only one thing that could make me even happier than I already was, and that was having the girl of my dreams back by my side. Having Jackie Dee at my side, even though it was just for that weekend, made it the best birthday I would ever come to celebrate. Thank you ever so much, Jackie Dee, for that weekend.

I continued to attend church, prayer meetings, and Bible studies. At each one of these gatherings, I never missed an opportunity to ask everyone to pray for Jackie. I asked everyone to pray that she would stop enjoying the things that were keeping us apart. In some cases, I would place Jackie's picture in the middle of the table along with everyone else's prayer requests, and then we would gather around these requests and offer up prayers for one another.

It seemed to be working too because Jackie started calling me up from the nightclubs and telling me that she was having a miserable time, but that she didn't know why. She said she just started feeling out of place, and she was getting tired of the same old bar scene routine. One time, Jackie called me up and said she was having such a miserable time that she wanted me to come and get her. The only problem was that she was so intoxicated that she didn't know which bar she was at. I kept Jackie talking on the telephone long enough for her to sober up and figure out which nightclub she was at.

Sometimes, Jackie would call me up from these places and tell me, "Don't you pray for me." Then she would get angry and say things like, "It won't bring me back to you, I'm divorcing you," and on and on. However, I never gave up hope, and one day Jackie called me up and said she needed to talk to me right away, then asked me if I could come over to her grandmother's house on Chelsea Street. I drove over there, and as I pulled up in front of the house, I could see Jackie standing there at the door and waiting for me. She let me in and said, "We need to talk; let's go upstairs."

Jackie led me through the house and took me upstairs and into the same room I used to climb up on the roof and through the window just five years earlier.

Then she told me that her parents had all the paperwork ready to be finalized on our divorce and that all she had to do was sign the papers to make it official. She also went on to say that she was involved with someone else and had been seeing him for a while now.

When Jackie told me all of this, there was only one question ringing in my mind that I did not ask her. Could the girl of my dreams really sign those papers that would separate her from the one person who absolutely loved, adored, and worshipped her? The answer was unequivocally—"NO!" Jackie said she could not go through with it, but she could not quite understand why. However, I knew. I believe she knew deep down in her heart that she would never find anyone in a thousand lifetimes who would ever cherish and adore her as much as I loved her. This kind of love does not exist except in this one very special and unique, once-in-a-lifetime relationship, and I'm referring to the love that I have always had for the girl of my dreams—Jackie Dee.

Jackie began to get tears in her eyes, and she hugged me around the neck. She said that she was confused and didn't know what to do about everything from her family pressuring her into divorcing me, to the relationship she was involved in, her drinking, and everything else. All I could say to Jackie was, "In a life full of uncertainties, if you remember nothing else, please remember this. There is only one thing in life that you can be absolutely certain of, and that is how I feel about you—girl. As far as everything else is concerned, it's a toss-up."

I asked Jackie if she would do something with me that I had never asked her to do before. I said, "Jackie, will you kneel down with me right now and pray with me about everything that is troubling you?" As the tears began to flow from our eyes, Jackie said in a soft voice, "Okay."

I took hold of both of her hands ever so gently, and we knelt down on the floor facing each other, and I began to pray for God's will in our lives. I prayed that God would give Jackie Dee the inner strength and confidence that he had given to me. I also prayed, "What God hath joined together, let not man put asunder," as the reverend had quoted to us during the exchange of our wedding vows four years earlier. Our hearts melted together right there on the floor as we knelt before God Almighty and pleaded with Him to save our marriage. Jackie and I even prayed that if it were possible, we would very much love to start a family, something that we had never been able to do before.

I could most definitely feel the hand of God sweeping over us as he was yet performing another miracle. You do not have to see God to know that he exists any more than you have to see the wind to know that it's real; we only see the effects of the wind. There is a mystery to it just like there is with God Almighty. God truly does work and move in mysterious ways.

This prayer that Jackie and I offered up to God took place on April 23 of 1982. From that day forth, Jackie and I were back together again, much to the chagrin of her family. On April 29 of 1982, Jackie committed her life to Christ and promised to be forever by my side. One month later, we conceived our first-born.

I have not had a drink of alcohol of any kind, taken any drugs, or even smoked a cigarette since the night of March 19, 1982, more than twenty-five years ago. Jackie Dee is still the only woman I have ever been with in my entire life. And after close to thirty years of marriage, I am still just as madly in love with her now as I always have been since that first day I saw her smile. The two of us have clung together tighter and tighter with each passing year. Our love for one another has reached new and greater heights in the last twenty-five years than I would ever have thought possible, and it is still expanding.

During these last twenty-five years of our marriage, Jackie has stood right by my side. No woman could ever have loved her man more than Jackie Dee has loved me.

She has given me everything that a woman could possibly give her man, and yet I feel like she has barely scratched the surface of what she has to offer me in the years to come, of the vast supply of love that is in her heart that she has been storing up for me. Jackie is the sum total of everything I could ever look for in a wife, lover, companion, and best friend.

To this day, I carry more than forty pictures of Jackie Dee in my wallet. I have no fewer than ten pictures of her on the night-stand beside my bed. I have pictures of her above the sun visor in my car. I have more than a dozen pictures of Jackie Dee on display in my workout room. Both of my computers at home and at work have hundreds of pictures, mostly of her, in a slide-show that flashes across the monitor when the system is in hibernation mode.

Everything that I am, everything about my identity, all of who and what I am is wrapped up and summed up in Jackie Dee. Without her, I am nothing. If I could open myself up to you and you could look into my soul, I am sure that you would see an image of Jackie Dee smiling that lovely and attractive smile of hers imprinted on my soul.

Although Jackie tells me often that she is just as much in love with me as I am with her, I have to scratch my head and wonder if that could ever be possible. What do you think?

The magic in her smile is still there after all these years.

The only dream I have ever had has been fulfilled.

In the end, for me, paradise had been restored. The girl of my dreams is back in my loving arms and will forever be by my side.

To Jackie Dee, the girl of my dreams, from the boy across the street: a promise is a promise. You are the only woman I have ever loved. I am yours now and forever. Your husband—Daniel

Epilogue

2 Corinthians 5:17: "Therefore if any man be in Christ, he is a new creation: old things are passed away; behold, all things are become new."

Matthew 19:26: "Jesus looked at them and said, 'With man this is impossible, but with God all things are possible.'"

I would be remiss if I did not take this opportunity to express my deepest regret to all those whom I may have offended in word or in deed at the times when I was lost in the early years of my life. I can only beg and plead most humbly for their forgiveness.

John 8:7: "He that is without sin among you, let him cast the first stone."

Romans 3:23: "For all have sinned, and come short of the glory of God."

As I have mentioned already—though I feel it warrants mentioning again—it gave me no earthly pleasure to write about things as sensitive, personal, and private as some of things I've written about here in this story. However, there was absolutely no way to leave out those portions of the story without it appearing full of holes and gaps, and yet be true and forthright with my story. As painful and unnerving as it was for me to do, I told this story from my heart. I hope it has touched those readers who took the time to pick it up off the shelf only to put it down and began reading its pages in positive way.

As I stated in the beginning of this book, numerous individuals have been telling me to write a book about my life for years, but I never felt compelled to do so until just recently when my younger brother Scott passed away. That experience taught me just how fleeting life can be, that and the passage of time from whence these events actually occurred seems ever quicker. I began to fear that I would pass out of this life without leaving behind some kind of legacy. I needed there to be a written testimonial of just how unparalleled and unprecedented my love has been for this most precious and lovely creature named Jackie Dee ever since I was a young boy.

Ironically enough, when I was ready to sit down and tell this story, over the next eighteen days I would estimate that 99 percent of the information contained in this book came to me in what can only be defined as a memory burst. Things I hadn't thought about for decades or thought that I had long since forgotten came back to me in clear and precise detail, and it had me literally reaching for pen and paper. By the eighteenth day, the memories from my past had ceased to surface.

This endeavor has been extremely helpful, to say the least, in helping me come to terms with my turbulent past and ease my conscience.

At this time, as I stand here on the threshold of turning fifty, I will make the following statement for the record:

It has been more than thirty-five years since the eyes of my heart were opened—triggered by Jackie Dee's smile on that most remarkable day. Since that day, my love for Jackie has not diminished in the slightest degree. To the contrary, it has flourished beyond measure to the point that I cannot stop thinking, talking, or writing about her; Heaven help me! There is nothing that excites me more than Jackie Dee's smile, the touch of her hand, and her warm embrace. Just the thought of her excites me so that I just can't sit still even to this very day, God help me!

Thank you, God, for bringing Jackie Dee into my life and for giving me a second chance.

Acts 2:21: "It shall come to pass that whosoever shall call upon the name of the Lord shall be saved."

It is between the blood of Christ and Jackie's love that empowers and encourages me to be all things that are good, wholesome, and pure—to her, my children, my grandchildren, and to be a benefit to everyone around me.

Jackie Dee 6

Jackie Dee Spring of '71

Jackie Dee 12

Jackie and Daniel '77

Jackie Dee 14

Aug 5ᵗʰ, 1978

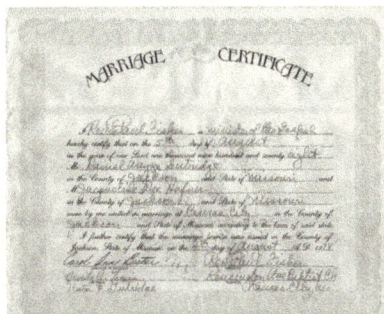

Marriage Certificate

Jackie & Daniel '80

Jackie Dee 18

Jackie and Daniel '82

Stephanie Renee

Tiffany Lynn

Daniel Jr.

Adrianna Chelsea

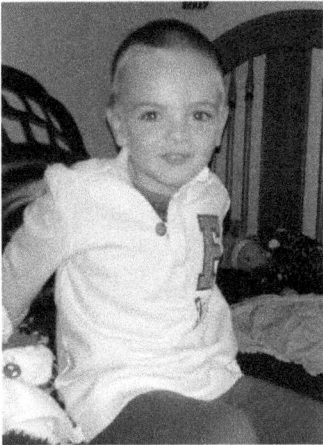

Tobias Niles

Jackie & Daniel